DOVER CASTLE

Dover Castle. *(English Heritage)*

DOVER CASTLE

ENGLAND'S FIRST LINE OF DEFENCE

ROY HUMPHREYS

The History Press

First published 2010
Reprinted 2014

The History Press
The Mill, Brimscombe Port
Stroud, Gloucestershire, GL5 2QG
www.thehistorypress.co.uk

British Library Cataloguing in Publication Data.
A catalogue record for this book is available from the British Library.

ISBN 978 0 7524 5550 1

Typesetting and origination by The History Press
Printed in Great Britain

CONTENTS

ROY S. HUMPHREYS
1928–2008

As a writer, Roy had a wonderful command of the English language. As a friend and colleague he could not be surpassed. It is all too tragic that having written this book on Dover Castle, he sadly never lived to see it in print.

At the request of Roy's wife, Hilda, I was happy to take on the task of bringing Roy's book to fruition. Dover Castle held a fascination for Roy and for many years he had considered a book about its history. I would like to thank Michelle Tilling for her help and guidance and The History Press for agreeing to take the book to print.

I am sure the memory of Roy will live on through this and the many other books that he wrote during his lifetime.

Robin J. Brooks
Aviation historian and writer

INTRODUCTION

Timeless and confident, Dover Castle stares down at us from its lofty perch, from where it has always captured the imagination, not least of the English, standing strong throughout centuries of political, social and economic conflict. It has stood for over nine hundred years, proudly symbolic of dogged resistance to anyone contemplating invasion of these shores. Perched on the white cliffs, the castle embodies the history of the land. It is the symbol of the nation's strength and the measure of her true greatness.

The rich history of Dover Castle, had we stood in the empty landscape before the Iron Age, would have been a glimpse into the future where all sorts of weird and wonderful things begin to happen. From the primitive age the landscape becomes deeply sinister. Looking at the white cliffs it is hard to know whether the chalk rock has been blasted into sculptured shapes by the sea and wind or has been cut into patterns. On reflection, there must have been occasions when the moon was full (or perhaps there was no moon at all, merely the light from burning torches) where, at the edge of the known world, with a sheer drop into the violent waves crashing against chalk rock below, sacrifices were probably made, praises uttered, or words said to pacify unforgiving gods. Evolution has continued apace over nine hundred years but although there have been adaptations of the existing site, it has rarely seen a multi-use other than its original concept.

From early Roman days, and onwards through the centuries, every new phase of our nation in the making has left its mark upon the castle. Successive invaders recognised that Dover was the key to these shores, and even the Saxons, who demolished or ruined most buildings they met with on their marches through Britain, spared some of the Roman work on Castle Hill.

A combination of Napoleonic and Second World War military tunnels beneath Dover Castle housed some of the most important battle rooms in recent British military history. These tunnels deep inside the famous white cliffs held secrets of over two centuries of military engineering techniques, and reveal 3½ miles of tunnels, chambers and vaults.

Sometimes, however, an awestruck visitor will begin to wonder whether it was ever the subject of some cataclysmic upheaval and, on closer inspection, there are indeed hints that all may not be as solid as we think. Far from being secured, the castle hides a labyrinth of tunnels beneath its apparently rock-solid facade. The military, over many years, have eaten away at the chalk foundations with intriguing results. There is no parallel in the British Isles where a castle is sitting on an extensive honeycomb of dark passages, tunnels and vaults, which seem to have no regard for any cultural architectural form.

Had English Heritage not seen the potential, the castle would still be the miserable, lack-lustre edifice of former years, its tunnels, chambers and vaults denied to the public, their history largely forgotten. Dover Castle is a survivor and remains intact in a way that represents as fundamental a part of English culture as our parish churches and cathedrals. It is to everyone's credit that we are able to cherish and celebrate its survival, despite the many years of profound economic and social change.

ONE

A FUSION OF CULTURES

History, like images, comes complete with its own landscape. Every landscape comes with its own set of meaningful images that today we see on the television screen. Doubtless the reader will have some knowledge of the subject so that when he comes across these images in their proper context they will not jar and falsify the moment.

Passive watching is an intense and private activity. It leaves a residue. The eyes look and take in these fleeting images, absorb them into a memory of something seen yesterday, a week ago, a decade past, or somewhere way back in the mists of time.

To put everything into perspective, the history of Dover Castle before the Roman invasion is not quite a blank page. The numerous tribes that inhabited Britain about 50 BC seem to have chiefly belonged to the Iberian race that passed through various stages of civilisation, and it was the Brythons (whose name Britain is derived from) whom the Romans first found in possession of the island when Julius Caesar arrived in 55 BC.

Wearing twisted gold necklaces and expertly worked bronze, they wore their hair long and used war chariots. They stained and tattooed their bodies, wore chequered cloth and ornamented rings on their fingers, and from their necks hung chains of brass or iron, suspended over their chests. A small shield, some sort of javelin or rounded sword was their arms, but although they exhibited considerable skill in warlike activities with neighbouring tribes, they had nothing that might be called a fortress. In general terms it was a domestic, social enclosure, wherein the privacy and property of its occupants was to be respected and protected by tribal law that existed at the time. It has been suggested therefore, that there is no evidence to show that a fortified residence was built there before the Roman Conquest.

Only a ditch defended their houses, chiefly clusters of wooden thatched huts, supported on stone foundations, and a rampart formed by timbers. Britons of the south-east had already begun to trade with the Continent, and were acquainted with metals, used gold coinage and were certainly partly civilised. The warlike inhabitants of the settlement, however, who confronted the Roman Legions, were not native Britons who, living further inland, were forest- and swamp-dwellers, living in small tribal-system communities. Existing Roman records mention an organised defence of these shores of such a formidable nature as to render the success of any landing doubtful. The strong warrior force they encountered, standing along the cliffs defiantly brandishing their spears and shields, meant they were obliged to sail to the flat shore further to the east.

It is reasonable to assume therefore, that England was 'colonised' from the Continent before Julius Caesar's time. That the coastal regions of Kent were in a more advanced state of civilisation than the inland portions of the county appears clear from the fact that Julius Caesar demanded and received grain from the defeated inhabitants in 54 BC. Although there is no doubt the Belgic tribe of East Kent resented Roman intrusion, they were prepared to continue their farming methods long after the conquest. The existing society and resources of the English Channel coastlands and the interior largely determined the course of the Roman Conquest and settlement in East Kent. The narrow sea, separating the island and mainland Europe, also determined that this should be the main factor of military invasion and the subsequent linkage with the Continent.

Three separate Roman military campaigns were set against Britain before the successful outcome of Claudius, who in AD 43 established a firm grip on East Kent before the legions pushed further north and west. Significantly, all three invasions, aimed at the coast between South Foreland and the mouth of the Wantsum Channel, took advantage of the Iron Age Belgic settlements on the rich lands they cultivated. In the years following the Claudian conquest, a Roman town of immense importance was established on the Belgic settlement, recorded as Durovernum, now Canterbury. In their magnificent road-building schemes connecting major ports and capitols, Dubris (Dover) was connected with Canterbury, as was Regulbium (Reculver), Rutupiae (Richborough) and Lemanis (Lympne), the latter a Roman naval base that later became a site of the Saxon Shore Fort in about AD 280.

As for Dover (Dubris), the closest sea route to the Continent, its prime function was largely confined to the military, diplomatic and administrative components of Imperial Rome. Recent archaeological evidence suggests the port was a chief naval base directly connected with Boulogne and, consequently, a quite different economic relationship endured with the pre-Roman population and its descendants with whom, out of necessity, there was a fusion of cultures.

In AD 43 the Emperor Claudius had deputed his greatest general, Aulus Plautius, to invade Britain and turn it into a Roman province. The whole venture was successful, and the Romans remained in the British Isles for nearly four hundred years. The army of occupation consisted of about four legions, one of which was stationed at (Dubris) Dover. Attached to this Legion was Publius Ostorius Scapula, who undoubtedly was the first architect of military works in the whole of England. During the years AD 43–50, Castle Hill was occupied and, towards the end of that period, two stone structures called the Pharos were constructed for use as beacons, for the guidance of shipping between the Continent and England, one on either side of the estuary.

It is impossible to say what other Roman buildings existed on Castle Hill at the time the Pharos were built, but it can be safely assumed that other buildings did exist for housing the legions, although there is no trace of their foundations today. Their demise is attributed to both the Saxons and the Normans who later dug out the foundations for their own building programme. The first line of defence of any invading army was to build a fortress on high ground to consolidate their advance and from this high point they could dominate local tribes and their chieftains.

The high ground on which the surviving Pharos stands was a point of natural military strength for defensive purposes and was probably the first work of the Roman garrison. Building the Pharos was a remarkable achievement, if only for the fact there is not one particle of English stone used in its construction. Practically all of the materials used were brought

The church of St Mary in Castro with the
Pharos beacon attached to it.

The Pharos beacon built by the Romans
is said to be the oldest in the country.

from the Continent, and this is one of the strongest grounds for suggesting that it is *the* oldest Roman building in England. It is open to conjecture whether they would have used Kent rag-stone instead of bringing material across the Channel had they known of its existence.

When the great Roman naval fort was built on top of the previous civil settlement beside the wide estuary below in about AD 270, local materials such as blocks of Calcareous Tufa and squared chalk blocks were used. The Pharos originally stood about 40ft high, the exterior being octagonal and the inside square. The walls were 10ft thick at the base and probably not quite as thick at the top. There were four floors, each approximately 14ft square. The materials used were a substance of volcanic origin, stone of a dense nature, tiles and shell mortar. Interestingly, the tiles are inscribed 'C L B R', a reference mark to the ships allotted for conveying materials and stores from the Continent to England. This surviving national monument has stood exposed to the prevailing south-westerly gales for more than 1,900 years.

Close to the Pharos stands the oldest church in England, a statement no doubt which will be contradicted, but the evidence in favour of its great antiquity seems overwhelming. That it might have been a barracks for the legions is undecided. The historical records of the Church of Rome provide convincing proof that a church existed within the defended limits of the fortress between the years 175 and 190. Lucius, who we might describe as a minor King of Kent, appears to have embraced a form of Christianity and started a campaign of conversion among the Roman soldiery. That he had a church, chapel or temple is made clear by the report of the visits of pilgrims. Whether Lucius raised a new building or adapted an existing pagan temple cannot be decided. But there is no doubt that evidence gleaned from documents suggests that in the year 200 a body of ecclesiastics had permanent residence near the church. That the church of that time was of the same style and dimensions as that which exists today is not asserted, but some portions of the original fabric stand and much of the original material in the building is indisputable.

After the Romans had evidently pacified the local inhabitants and felt more secure from attack, they paid less attention to the defences on Castle Hill than to those on the shore below between the prominent cliffs. From the earliest date of their occupation they feared the raiding sea-parties from the more northern Teuton territories, and concentrated their efforts on defending this chief port with the Continent. As the centuries passed the sea raiding became bolder, and pillaging settlements on both sides of the Channel became a menace to the power of Rome. The Emperor Constantine, in order to counter these activities, formed several legions to garrison the ports, and brought into being a commander known as the 'Count of the Saxon Shore'.

This high official took up residence in Dover, and as a result of his presence and that of his minor court, Dover became a place of great importance. The chronicled definite figures of the Dover garrison suggests a strength in excess of 1,200 men, of which no less than two Roman centuries would be on duty at the shore forts. This would perhaps suggest that at least half the troops were stationed on what is now known as Castle Hill.

Of all the coastal towns in East Kent, Dover has the longest and most interesting history. The Dour Valley was the only break in the long line of chalk cliffs which once formed an inlet of the sea, an estuary occupied in Neolithic and Iron Age times. More importantly two Roman forts have been uncovered almost on top of each other. The earliest dates from the second century when Dubris was an important naval base serving the Roman Fleet – the Classis Britannica – whose galleys patrolled the Dover Strait and the Channel.

Especially charged to defend the Gallic and British shore against the plundering Saxon pirates was Carausius, who from about AD 286 to 293 ruled the island as an independent sovereign, safe behind his own navy. He has been recognised as the first sea king of Britain, just before the province of Roman Britain was to enjoy a last golden age. The Count of the Saxon Shore defended the coast from the Wash to Portsmouth, aided by ten large fortresses, of which Richborough was the most important. Each of the fortresses, Dover being the next westward, had a fleet of ships, which could – and did – intercept and fight invaders at sea. By this method the inhabitants were reasonably secure from Saxon attack for at least another half century. Through Dover at this time, grain, cloth and even jewellery was being sold to the Continent which probably implies that prosperity and the economic situation in Britain was as good if not better than other provinces of the Roman Empire. The later fort, dating from the third century, forms part of the network of the defensive sea base known as 'Forts of the Saxon Shore'. Recent excavations reveal a substantial Roman house with wall paintings and, with the two lighthouses (Pharos) on both the north and south cliffs, Dover can claim to have as varied a collection of Roman antiquities as any other town in the south-east of England. Although there is little tangible evidence of the Saxon period at Dover, there is no doubt that the port was used by them long before the inlet silted up.

But in the last half of the fourth century the downfall began. Life and property became insecure when raiding Saxons swarmed, at first, into areas of un-Romanised districts. The heart of the Roman Empire was weakened by these attacks on the home front and it has been suggested that the inferior soldiers and civilians who had arrived from the Continent to serve in Britain were the cause. Even before the final Saxon onrush had finally destroyed the Latin influence on the island, a Celtic revival had already begun elsewhere.

In the first fifty or so years of the fifth century, Romanised Britain found itself alone in its defence strategy, quite unsupported by the once-awesome Empire. The barbarous Saxons became the chief instruments in the destruction of Roman Britain. They came over the sea in increasing numbers and boldness to settle in a land rich in grain fields, pasture and broadleaf forests swarming with deer and swine. But the advanced guard were bloodthirsty pirates, happy to destroy a higher civilisation than their own. Had they not been so barbarous they would not have destroyed the Roman civilisation. The Saxon ideology, such as it was, was merely basic. After all, if you pillage and rape the land and its peoples you are surely defeating your own object in domineering them. Putting down those who resist is perhaps understandable but to get rid of a skilled workforce means you will have to work the plough yourself. The deckless shallow-draught Saxon galleys were rowed upstream on rivers, deeper and more navigable than they are today, into the interior to take the inhabitants by the sword. Once the Roman military system was undermined by this method of infiltration, the Roman road system only served to hasten the pace of conquest and destruction.

The Roman port of Dubris, one imagines, should have been able to use its disciplined infantry, clothed in body armour and using modern weaponry of the later Roman period, against the warlike Saxon warriors who used inferior weapons. Historians are not sure if the defenders fought principally in Roman or Celtic fashion, but whatever method they used the Romans were conquered by the Saxons who, unbelievably, had neither discipline, barracks, body armour or heavy weapons. Their main advantage, it has been suggested, was energy and purpose. The Roman defenders possessed a formidable fortress on Castle Hill, with its steep earthworks surrounding the stockades. Below were the once-immaculate stonewalled buildings of the Classis Britannica port. However, surprisingly, the partially armed barbaric warriors, coming ashore from their long-ships, destroyed these obstacles one by one.

Perhaps the peculiarity of the later Roman system in the south and east of the island largely depended on untrained citizens who, unlike the feudal lords of later times, were never fighting men, had no training and no fortified mansions. If the Roman world was more civilised than the medieval, it was proportionally more incapable of local self-help. Everywhere, in the many history books we read of the Saxons' pillage, rape and plunder, it is suggested that each historian has assumed the priest Gildas' *Book of Lamentations* in Latin to be accurate. As it was written one hundred years after the events described, its accuracy is in question. Whatever view one takes there is the certainty that the heathen Saxons destroyed Roman Britain.

From a thriving Roman Port, Dubris experienced the wanton destruction of the Roman villas beside the River Dour. The Saxon was not a town dweller and the only mercantile instincts he possessed were selling slaves to the Continent. Eventually, however, the more domesticated Saxons were to arrive in greater numbers who settled in the rural areas to till the soil on the open-field system. This became the basis of the English civilisation. Ignoring the Roman stone buildings in abundance with all their modern conveniences, they confusingly built log houses grouped around a large log hall. Split trunks of forest timber, set vertically side-by-side, formed the walls and, as recent archaeology suggests, when the forests were depleted and timber became scarce they began to build the half-timber frame, in-filled with stonework.

It is perhaps difficult to exaggerate the injury done to Roman Britain, and in a generation or two the arts and traditions that once enabled them to look down upon the Saxons were forgotten. They lost the crafts, science and learning of Rome. In Saxon England, Christian religion and Romano-Celtic language disappeared, together with the Roman administrative boundaries and, as towns and villages changed their names, Dubris became Dover. The whole gamut of change also implies a rapid change in racial stock.

Perhaps the greatest disaster that ever happened to this country was the departure of the Romans in AD 410. The day Dover saw the sailing of the last cohort marked the start of one of the blackest periods in the history of England. The Romanised inhabitants of Kent fought bravely and successfully for over forty-five years against successive invaders until finally, in AD 457, the Jutes completed the conquest of Kent by the capture of Richborough and Dover. Bad as the plight of the town in 457 was, still worse was to come twenty years later when the Saxons fought their way along the Kent coast and slew the inhabitants of towns and largely demolished all the shore-line forts and most of the defences.

Hengist the Jute stands as the chief warrior who became the basis of aristocracy and feudalism of the English and, perhaps unwittingly, founded England and all that has become of England since. The bones of these warrior chiefs, when excavated today, are surrounded by their iron spearheads, bosses and handles of the round wooden shields and small hand axes. Some of these great unknowns – men of action rather than genius – must have known Dover. It is lamentable that true life stories of any one of these is not recorded, which would tell why they and their men decided to cross the sea, where they landed and how they fought, wrought and thought; the past is inexorable in its silence. There are few early authentic chronicles of the

Saxon Conquest. The heathen Saxon invaders had a runic alphabet that appears on sword or stone but it was never used to record their deeds.

The Saxon-Celtic barbarism did not begin to emerge into the twilight of history until St Augustine and his monks brought back with them the Latin alphabet and the custom of a written record. Between these points, however, stretches a great chasm of darkness and the most important page of our national history remains blank. In the early days before the Roman invasion of the British Isles, various strongholds or fortifications were erected around large towns or burghs as a defensive measure. It is indisputable that an Iron Age settlement was established at Dover on Castle Hill and it follows that the resident lord or chieftain would have occupied it as it looked down upon the town.

It would appear the Saxons did pay some regard to the value of the Castle Hill defences and maintained the deep Roman ditches and wooden palisades and buildings within the boundary. They also, undoubtedly, dug themselves caves in the chalk strata. That the defences fell into the hands of successive invaders during this period and afterwards is uncertain, although most historians would agree that very little distinction is to be made between Saxon, Angle, Jute and Dane, and that the difference was provincial rather than national.

There is no doubt that the settlement was a product of feudalism, a symbol of feudal lordship, finding its origin in the ninth and tenth centuries establishing a feudal society that was prevalent throughout Europe. In about AD 600 the Saxons are, surprisingly, attributed with building the first wall round the top of the old Roman earthworks, composed of various crude forms of stone and flint. The ditches or moats were dug deeper which made formidable obstacles to any attacker. The wall was extended and strong gates added, and within the boundary there would have been secure places for their horses, domestic animals, workshops and forges – in fact, a self-contained community using a local labour force to sustain the whole concept.

An authentic reference to Dover Castle is made in about AD 590 when Ethelbert, King of Kent, retired within its defences on the occasion he was harassed by a neighbouring chieftain. In about AD 597 he received there, and allowed to there remain St Augustine, sent by Pope Gregory from Rome. He was given a piece of land just outside Canterbury and built an abbey; the St Augustine Abbey site is probably the oldest in England. In about 597, St Augustine preached the Gospel, re-converted Kent and re-consecrated the church within the castle boundary, which, it has been suggested, probably took the form of a cross at that time.

Probably the whole of Kent had embraced Christianity in 696, and the newly appointed Archbishop of Canterbury, Theodore, visited the clerics housed in Dover where, it is believed, he attended services with the canons in the castle. For nearly a century the church was in regular use, but in 696 the canons and ecclesiastics were removed from the castle to the town and the church fell into disrepair through disuse.

Dover was becoming a place of much importance during the ninth century, and Castle Hill was being made into a formidable stronghold. Towards the end of the century the Danes made several attacks on the Kent coast, but despite several successes elsewhere, when they captured Canterbury they failed in their efforts to seize Dover.

At the death of Edward the Elder in 924, his legitimate son being too young, the crown passed to his illegitimate son Athelstan to whose accession no opposition was made. The whole of England from the English Channel to the Forth fell under Athelstan who, rather than his grandfather Alfred the Great, merits the title of first King of England. He established a close connection with the nearest parts of the Continent and encouraged commerce and enacted many laws for this end, one of which conferred the title of Thane on any merchant who had made three voyages to the Continent in his own ships.

In about 1020 Godwin was created Earl of Wessex, and he, perhaps more than his successors, should be given the credit of appreciating the strategic value of Dover and the importance of adequately guarding the gateway of England. During the thirty-two years he had held sway in the south of England and was the adviser of kings, Kent and Sussex became exceedingly prosperous; of which prosperity he took full toll. He was a hard, overbearing man and quite ruthless in his methods, but he had many good points, not least, to fight to the last for those associated with him. Although he practically enslaved the local population in strengthening the fortress walls, building guardrooms and loopholes, erecting massive gates and towers for watchmen and even a keep with a wall of masonry around it, he nevertheless defended the townspeople against his king – Edward the Confessor. At that time Dover was one of the five original Cinque Port towns created by Edward the Confessor. The Dover fleet of ships was given royal patronage when Edward sought protection from the piratical intrigue of local mariners. The town was required to supply ships and their crews to defend the coast as it had done under the Saxon dynasty.

Legend suggests that when Eustace, Count of Boulogne and husband of the king's sister, was passing through Dover to visit the Court of London, a quarrel arose between some of his men and the townspeople. From the *Anglo-Saxon Chronicle* of 1051 we read that Count Eustace and his followers 'went up to the burgh (castle) and slew more than twenty men.' Angry burghers drove them from the town, but later, on his return to France, he had demanded from the local townspeople food and accommodation for his numerous knights, soldiers and servants. There have been crucial moments in our history when the so-called powerless gathered together in sufficient numbers to form a power-base which became more potent than any force in this land or any other. The townspeople refused to assist him. They armed themselves and, assisted by the castle garrison, inflicted heavy casualties on the count's men. The king thereupon ordered Godwin to take vengeance on the town and execute all who had taken part in the affair. This Godwin refused to do. The earldom of this great man extended from Kent to Wessex and he even went to the extreme measure of raising a force against the king.

Following the death of Godwin in 1052, his son Harold became Earl of Wessex. He, like his father, maintained the fortress in good condition and kept it garrisoned. The origin of the castle, so it has been said, owes itself to a French innovation and, more especially, a Norman importation. However, Dover Castle was known all over the Continent as a stronghold of great importance, and it is perhaps open to conjecture whether too much credit has been given to the Normans for its strength at a later date, and too little credit given to the English earls before the Norman Conquest. The castle was basically a fortified residence for the lord or chieftain, baron or king. Although it has been asserted that a masonry keep never existed in Saxon times at Dover, there exists the old chronicles that refer to Earl Godwin employing masons and artisans to build towers and strengthen the castle and it particularly mentions a keep. For a period prior to 1066 there had been more or less free intercourse between the Continent and England, so it is hardly feasible to ascribe work to the year of the succession of a Norman king, when the workmen and artisans from the Continent came and went freely many years before.

TWO

FRENCH-SPEAKING BARONS

Since monarchs were not yet chosen in a strict order of heredity, the childless Edward had included William, Duke of Normandy, as a possible successor to the throne of England. However, when Edward had nominated Harold, son of Godwin, as heir to the kingdom, William felt slighted and almost at once prepared for an invasion of England.

William the Conqueror, in his claim to the English throne, was crowned at Westminster on Christmas Day 1066. He had made references to the castle at Dover with its keep building and well, and further reference is made in the *Anglo-Saxon Chronicle* to the apartments in the keep. Therefore, there is evidence that a keep structure was in existence long before the erection of the Norman keep. Before this period, however, the Saxons, we have learned, built several crude towers on the outer defence ditches, and two towers also stood on the site of the present King's Gate. There was also a towered entrance at Colton's Gate, and two or three drawbridges were in existence from small towers or outworks.

With the new monarchy there spread also a new feudalism of a professional military nature. Huge earth mounds were built by forced peasant labour throughout the land, upon which were erected the timber fortresses, although Dover's mound on Castle Hill was already in place. Interestingly, recent archaeological work suggests that the Normans actually added to the pre-existing Iron Age fortification in about eight days. Its motte, the mound of excavated soil piled up in solidly compacted layers, and the large cleared area known as the bailey, was already an impregnable citadel from which Norman horsemen set out to dominate the countryside, not only to pursue law and order, but often to plunder wealthy landowners and seize their plots of fertile land.

By the end of 1068 William was recognised as the true lord in southern England and, with few exceptions, was acknowledged elsewhere as king. He put an end to most of those old-fashioned liberties of Danelaw and promptly imposed the French system of strictly territorial feudalism. Inevitably Saxon ideas and civilisation, such as it was, gave way to Norman. In the south-east, where the economic progress of its peoples depended largely on Continental trade, it was still an aggregation of races, regions and private jurisdictions, which needed to be amalgamated into one nation. The Normans were the new masters who would do it.

The Norman Conquest, like that of the Roman, proved valuable to England. One major factor was to strengthen the king who, though nominally elected, was practically absolute.

A baron of the eleventh century. William the Conqueror arrived in 1066 and was pleased to have the voluntary help of barons and knights, not only from Normandy, but from Brittany and Flanders as well.

The Normans improved the administration systems and for many years Norman French was the language of the court and the upper echelons of society, with peasant English being spoken by the rest. However, the language barrier served to widen the gulf between the French-speaking aristocracy and the peasantry.

Eight Norman Knights were associated with Dover Castle in particular: John de Fiennes, William d'Avranches, Fulbert de Lucy (later changed to Dover), William d'Arsick, William de Peverel, Walkelin Magminot, Robert de Porth, and Robert de Crevequer. The knight evolved into an exclusive class of warrior; not only a new military elite but also becoming a social elite – their social status strengthened when they received grants of land from their lord. Land was then the principle form of wealth and it follows that they held a parcel of land in return for their services. The feudal lord had the right to demand from the knight to attend military service.

Simon, heir of William d'Avranches, also succeeded him to become the defender of Rochester Castle against King John in 1202, on the surrender of which he was taken prisoner and remained so until the fifth year of Henry II's reign. Matilda, his daughter, whose brother William had not survived his father, carried the barony six years afterwards in marriage to Hamo de Crevequer, the Great Baron of Kent. The family of Crevequer resided at Leeds Castle, their barony, like that of the d'Avranches, was held by the castle guard tenure of Dover Castle. Their son Robert, also one of the knights associated with the defence of Dover, had a tower named after him. Hamo de Crevequer had, like the rest of the knights, accompanied William the Conqueror to England and became steward of his household and Sheriff of Kent for life. The wealthy family of Hamo de Crevequer was involved in the disagreement with Simon de Montfort but his family became extinct in the reign of Edward I, his son dying without issue.

In a land full of armed, French-speaking barons accustomed to maintaining their rights and privileges by the sword, they were confident in retaining their privileges usually enjoyed on the Continent. Some of them turned with fury upon William when they realised the restrictions he had imposed upon their power. In the last years of William's reign he was frequently called upon to suppress their enthusiasm for their causes. The lower echelon Anglo-Saxons had been schooled to suffer the tyranny of the strong even under their native rulers. The barons' rising of 1075 and its prompt suppression by the king shows that the Norman Conquest was well and truly complete.

Before the Norman invasion the Saxons had their first line of defence of Castle Hill on the outer extremity of the moat or ditch, where they had hewn from the chalk various observation posts and connecting passages. The main entrance, connecting with the town below and leading to a gate in the town wall, was in an area we now know as Canons' Gate. William had shared a common boundary in France with the Count of Anjou, so it was inevitable they all should refurbish their stone defences. The construction of a new fortress of stone for military purposes, as well as for their own egos, resulted in the great medieval strongholds which survive today. Building this Norman stronghold was most probably achieved by Fulbert de Lucy, one of William's foremost supporters and whose name he later changed to Fulbert de Dover. He had been given the Manor of Chilham and was granted permission to build a castle there, he also having connection with William's system of castle guard tenure. He was one of the eight knights holding lands in exchange for castle guard tenure and who held between them knight's fees for the defence of Dover Castle.

The architectural development of Dover Castle from the Norman period saw, undoubtedly, the beginning of the English castles in this country. Materials used later and in more permanent construction work, inevitably, re-used blocks, bricks and tiles from the many ruins of old Roman buildings. The Anglo-Saxon craftsmen were splitting local rag-stone instead, although they had re-used Roman tiles to form several door arches. Interestingly, the sometimes-crude Saxon building methods seem to have continued long after William's arrival and well into the twelfth century.

The English castle was built by these Norman men and placed in the hands of reliable custodians whose loyalty to the king was unquestionable. When the Constable's Tower was built in Henry III's reign, only persons of some importance were allowed to use it until much later, when the marshal used it to levy his tolls upon all traders entering. The first marshal of the castle was Hugh de Beauchamp who kept lists of everyone connected with the garrison, their work and pay and was given the responsibility to organise the guards and watchmen. In addition he also purchased food and wine, forage for the animals and dealt with both the military and civil offenders who flouted the laws. A form of taxation was also introduced upon all tradesmen serving the castle garrison, victualling merchants, craftsmen, artisans, saddlers, tailors and barbers. In fact, anyone who worked for or supplied the garrison was required to pay the sum of four pence per week.

One of the marshal's most important duties was making arrangements for visiting monarchs. He had the privilege of being in attendance at the throne and all-important functions in the area, not least being Master-at-Arms during bouts and duels, a form of entertainment that befitted a king, when knights and town freemen were often persuaded to challenge each other on the cleared bailey area. Trial by combat, arranged by the king, was a sort of jurisprudence, which the feudal barons could administer as a proud privilege in executing justice. Each combatant had to stake his life and his honour upon the truth of his declaration, knowing that if he failed he would be dishonoured. Of course, as few of the barons were literate, the judicial combat was more likely an event in which to settle disagreements as opposed to the obvious, more administrative alternative.

The Norman Conquest did not destroy or abolish all the existing laws or institutions but influenced them until gradually the whole was preserved. Feudalism was the organisation of society according to certain ideas; for example all land was held by grant from the king and for such a grant, military service and payment of dues were required. In practice, the great Norman baron landowner, who had obtained the wealth of England and also held land on the Continent, aimed to secure independence within their estates in Britain. The right of private war and the right of private coinage reduced royal power to a mere shadow. William developed a feudal

The tournament, a form of entertainment that befitted a king, was usually held in the Northfall Meadow beside the castle.

idea in the system in which there was a regular hierarchy of barons, knights, freeholders and villeins, with the king as lord paramount. Later, combat duels became an entertainment of kings rather than a means of settling disputes and maintaining one's honour. It was wholly distinct from the lawless encounters which took place among the chivalry of feudal times.

For most of the twelfth century, the English Channel was an Anglo-Norman sea, especially under Henry I who became king in 1100. On this water sailed ships of the Cinque Ports, bridging the two communities of England and France and sharing the same sovereign.

At Dover Castle, according to the plans of Gundulf, a militant bishop, the huge keep we see today was almost certainly started in the reign of Henry I in the year 1133, and was probably not finished until 1188. It still retains its original architectural features despite the many alterations made in the course of nine centuries, which most often were enlargements

The jousts were a more personalised combat and were usually between knights and freemen. Each combatant staked his life and his honour upon the truth of his declaration.

Burgess' romanticised painting of Dover Castle gives an artistic view of how the castle looked before the castellation was removed.

of windows and the occasional removal of interior masonry to make rooms larger and lighter. The keep is typically Norman in design and is mirrored in many other similar eleventh- and twelfth-century buildings such as the Tower of London, Arundel, Hedingham and Rochester. Generally speaking, the internal arrangements are more or less to the same exact specifications, with one or more large halls on the first and second floors approached by a stone staircase, with an additional circular stairway also serving them. The intimidating keep at Dover is one of the finest examples left unspoiled in England.

The curtain wall which encloses the keep, however, through several alterations to the fabric over many years, has lost most of its original romantic, crenellated architectural design that we associate with castles. The foundations of the keep are set on solid chalk rock, which give a wall thickness of about 22ft, supporting the 96ft high towers; while below the elegant stairway there is about 40ft of solid masonry. This formidable strength made the keep insurmountable to would-be attackers, although it has been suggested that, despite the large area covered by the building, the ground floor space was hardly adequate to sustain the defenders. Three separate ways, a drawbridge, huge doors and a grille, originally defended the grand stairway, while halfway up and concealed from the entrance there was a gallery for archers and, much later, musketeers. The banqueting halls are large and originally would have had timber roofing, later converted to brick vaulting which unfortunately, concealed the fine galleries that ran around them, leaving only the minstrels' gallery in situ.

The medieval Dover Castle hides a labyrinth of tunnels, dark passages and vaults beneath its apparently rock-solid façade. *(Simmons Aerofilms Ltd.)*

Looking into the past through an imaginary eye, we can see inside the bailey where there stood a vast, rough-hewn wooden wheel, similar to a water wheel. Attached to it, by various wooden cogs and pulleys, was a great timber lever. With two men standing inside the wheel treading wooden planks, the huge contraption could lift upwards of 2 tons. Men in homespun cloth tunics and wearing leather boots led horses pulling cartloads of rough-hewn stone. The stone, chiselled into square blocks, had been largely excavated from local quarries, although some of it had come from as far away as the Maidstone area. The blocks were taken to the stonemasons who, under the watchful eye of the master mason, chipped away at each block until it became smooth. When lifted into place, the blocks were bedded-in with a lime and

25

St John's Tower (in the foreground) is at the extreme north-west of the castle boundary. Originally it had three separate levels, the lowest of which led to the many tunnels hewn out of the chalk. One actually runs beneath the Deal Road.

This is St John's Tower showing the trapdoor leading to a lower level.

sand mortar mixture. Close by was the forge where iron nails were made, used to fix the timber palisades and the stout timber poles that rose into the sky beside the massive walls. When finished, the whole structure with its many towers would look down upon a dry moat, which any invader would have to cross under a hail of arrows fired from the battlements.

There are two Norman chapels. The first and lower of the two is St John's, and was most probably used as a general place of worship, while St Thomas's, with an ante-chapel, on the ground floor above, was probably used by the more important officials. Religious observance of the Norman soldiery was of paramount importance and punishments were enacted upon those who failed to comply with orders, especially in the failure to keep the chancel lights burning.

The constable appointed the domestic structure within the keep, the warders, sergeants, cooks and the umpteen servants. Of the two halls, the large banqueting hall was undoubtedly the more important, having a ladies' gallery at one end with a retiring room leading from it. The second hall held the royal apartments and was conveniently situated so that the more important people could have access to the chapel and ladies' gallery without going through the main hall. Interestingly, the Normans built the well supplying water, although some experts suggest it was originally either Roman or Saxon.

It is perhaps as well to review the influence of religion on the castle's welfare under the Saxons. Prior to the accession to power of Godwin, the religious orders held great sway for a period of nearly a century, and had at least two chapels within the castle. The clerics undoubtedly had a monastery attached to these chapels, and it has been suggested that a guarded nunnery also existed there. Godwin, however, made a clean sweep of all religious orders from within the defended area and it was not until 1051, after Godwin's banishment, that Edward the Confessor restored the old church, reinstated some of the clerics, endowed it with lands and appointed and regulated certain church functions in connection with the castle garrison. It is quite probable that it was in this period that the church took on its present dimensions and architectural characteristics, as reliable records exist to the effect that masons and artisans were obtained from the Continent for rebuilding this church and others in Kent during the great religious revival. The sites of some of the buildings that housed the clerics and nuns were probably where the Georgian Officers' Mess building stands today.

The English Church suffered the same fate as the English aristocracy when William deposed at least five bishops in 1070. William's men replaced them and Lanfranc became the new Archbishop of Canterbury. By 1096 there was not one single bishopric in English hands.

THREE

DEVICES OF WARFARE

When William the Conqueror arrived in 1066, Dover Castle was practically denuded of men and had to surrender to his superior army after a sharp fight. William's Normandy was of small but powerful feudal states and he had carefully prepared his invasion by using diplomacy, propaganda and a unique spy system. It was an enterprise far beyond his resource and so he elected to recruit barons and their men-at-arms. Although he had no feudal law to call on barons to help with his campaign, he was nonetheless pleased to have the voluntary help

The armoury in the Great Hall was an impressive sight to the visitor but it became corroded by sea air and had to be removed. *(Dover Museum)*

of barons and knights from not only Normandy but from Brittany and Flanders. They owed no allegiance except to serve under his banner but they, in turn, were hopeful of obtaining the wealth of England, its lands and precious metals.

It has been estimated that 12,000 men, of whom probably less than half were cavalry, with perhaps 5,000 knights, eventually subdued, robbed and permanently held sway over the English. This gives some understanding of the political and military backwardness of the Anglo-Saxon system compared with the Norman.

The main
stairway from the
Great Hall.
(Dover Museum)

Norman knights and English housecarls wore much the same armour while the cavalry, to provide a split skirt for convenience of the rider, only lengthened the primitive ring-mail outer garment of their common ancestry. Both sides wore the conical helmet and protective nosepiece that were then in fashion, and their shields were the pointed kite shape, long and tapering to protect the wearer's thighs when on horseback. The Norman cavalry fought from the saddle, casting and thrusting with their long, heavy spear or striking downwards with their heavy sword. They had not only learned of cavalry tactics from the French, but they had also preserved the old Scandinavian practice of archery, which the Anglo-Danes had neglected. The English were exposed to the archers, inferior to the later longbowmen of Crécy, but at the time, superior to English bowmen on that day.

The Norman king immediately garrisoned the castle with a sufficient number of trusted followers to hold his line of retreat open when advancing on London. He also left in the castle his sick and wounded and caused certain reinforcements, servants and workmen to be brought there from his Duchy of Normandy. The wisdom of William in thus securing Dover was shown when the rising in Kent against his rule occurred a year later. William had returned to Normandy in February 1067 leaving his half-brother Odo, Bishop of Bayeux, in complete charge. Odo crushed everyone in his ruthless determination to bring the country to heel and made such heavy exactions upon the population of the county that the more disgruntled barons promised the Count Eustace of Boulogne large payments and privileges if he would come over and assist them in driving Odo out. Eustace sent over men and stores and succeeded to pacify the population until he attempted to besiege the castle, where he was repelled.

When William returned to England in 1085, with a vast army of mercenaries ready to counter the suspected invasion of King Swein of Denmark, he thought it prudent to have more precise information about the wealth of his barons. The result was the inquiries of the Domesday Book of 1086.

William found the castle a useful stronghold and attached so much importance to it that he appointed his brother Odo as Constable of the Castle, the first in the long line of constables, also creating him Earl of Kent and Lord Chief Justice of England. On his appointment, Odo was given an assistant, William Fitz-Osborn, who surveyed the fortifications and organised a defence structure. The Normans expressed their power in stone, building castles, the likes unseen before (ninety of them were built), and stone churches in villages while, in what became cities, they built vast cathedrals. The relics of the Norman Conquest are everywhere.

The strengthening of the defences proceeded to a set plan, which had for its chief object the building of an outer ring of towers and small forts, largely supported by knights who were given land in various parts of the country as a reward for building and manning the towers and forts situated on the ramparts.

Starting from Canons' Gate, it has an arched entrance with a drawbridge, defended by two small stone towers with battlements. Rokesley's Tower, although built by Albrincis, was actually manned by Thomas de Rokesley, after whom it is named. Between this tower and the old Canons' Gate entrance, several small buildings were built for the accommodation of the defenders, which most probably included quarters for the knights when in residence. Fulbert de Dover's Tower is a square tower built by Fulbert de Lucy, who later changed his name. This is the site of the old prison in which, from time to time, many leading merchants of Dover were

This 1844 painting by Burgess shows the Well Tower, later demolished to make way for the Victoria barracks. *(Dover Museum)*

Peverell's Tower.

incarcerated for non-payment of debts and fines. Next is Hirst's Tower, a circular tower built by Fulbert de Dover but defended by John de Hirst. Say's Tower was built by William de Arsick and actually defended by him, although at one time Jeffrey de Say commanded it. De Say was thought to have been a constable at one time during the constableship of John de Fiennes and, for whatever reason, de Say's name seems to have been handed down and given to the tower.

Peverell's Tower has had several names, including 'Beauchamp' and 'Marshal'. It is a fine example of Norman defence architecture which, although being an outer-work fortification, could quite easily be used as an inner defence in the event of the enemy penetrating between Canons' Gate and itself. The tower and gateway were built on the site of an Old Saxon fortification and joined the two wall flanks running down from the keep and Constable's Tower. The defenders were so placed that they could command the dry moat area north and south and also the approaches from the direction of Canons' Gate and Constable's Tower, and seaward there was a moat with a drawbridge across the present road. Within the tower were several apartments where the marshal, the constable's right-hand man, was also housed. Later, a caponier (a sort of covered passage) was built from the tower to the Palace Gate entrance to the keep.

Queen Mary's Tower was built by Hugh de Port and is entirely different in design from any other. This crenellated tower has been known by the names 'Port' and 'Gosling', the former being the surname of its builder, and the latter from the name of the knight who was subsidised

The keep with the Victoria barracks on the right, now demolished.

with land-tenures to provide men to defend it. During Queen Mary's reign, the tower fell into a state of disrepair, and from the fact that the queen defrayed the costs of restoration, it has from that time borne her name.

Constable's Tower has a fine and imposing entrance, somewhat marred by the addition of brickwork, but even today it makes a splendid picture for any artist. The second constable, John de Fiennes, who succeeded Odo, built the gateway, towers and residence. This entrance was the first made into the castle that was in any way spacious. A tower was built on each side of the gateway while a few years later a second tower was added to the north side. A drawbridge with the extra protection of a portcullis and massive gates crossed the dry moat. The apartments were far more salubrious than in any other building in the castle at the time and much later two wings were added within the arch to increase accommodation and so make a suitable residence for the deputy constable, whose title usually goes with the Command of Dover Garrison. Even later, the Lord Warden of the Cinque Ports is, by virtue of such appointment, also Constable of Dover Castle.

Built by John de Fiennes and defended by Clopton, after whom it is named, Clopton's Tower was later named Treasurer's Tower, being used in feudal times as a pay office for tolls, fines, hiring and emoluments. Interestingly, it served at various times as a wardrobe-room for visiting sovereigns.

Although built by Fulbert de Dover, taking its name from Godfoe who later defended it, a small tower exists under the latter name.

Robert Crevecoeur, son of one of William I's strongest supporters (de Crevequer), built Crevecoeur's Tower. His father, for services rendered, was appointed Sheriff of Kent for life, and theirs was, for many years, a very important family – one of his descendants became Great Baron of Kent.

Gilbert de Magminot, a great favourite of William I and a knight of some importance and influence and who also became Marshal of the Castle, built the Norfolk Tower.

There were originally three separate towers joined by a strong curtain wall, and the whole made an extremely strong work at the time. In Norman times, and up to the middle of the eighteenth century, because of the high ground in front of it, it was considered the best spot for an attack.

The strong Fitzwilliam's Tower had an entrance beneath it. A masonry passage led through the moat and under the outer bank into Northfall Meadow. All the entrances were strongly defended, and there existed various devices to trap unauthorised entrants. Included also was a massive gate, drawbridge and portcullis.

The Avranches Tower is one of the most interesting buildings, strongly occupying a corner of the curtain wall. The arches and staircase are finely designed and give a good idea of the splendid masonry work of the later Norman period, having three floors with battlements for observation purposes.

Pencester's Tower was another entrance strongly defended by a tower with the usual Norman devices of drawbridge and gates. It has been suggested this was an early Saxon entrance strengthened by Earl Godwin at a much later date. Three further towers were built into the curtain wall but, as it was one of the most difficult areas to approach, the Ashford Towers, as they were known, were only lightly defended. St John's Tower formed the main entrance and had three levels, each with distinctive Norman arch ceilings.

The Avranches Tower.

Colton Tower, now demolished.

An early passage beneath Dover Castle.

These Norman passages may have been cut to allow the garrison to leave the castle under siege. There are umpteen others that have never been found. It is thought Hubert de Burgh was responsible in the reign of King John.

The old Saxon Gate, said to be one of the oldest buildings in the country.

At the lowest level there exist many chalk-hewn passages branching off in so many directions as to suggest they had led to either the keep or Constable's Tower. An even deeper series of passages lie beneath a trap door. Tunnels of labyrinthine proportions were under the moats and ditches and one in particular, with a 200-yard-long gallery, ran beneath what is now the Deal Road, where circular shafts in the ceilings led to a series of chambers above.

In both Saxon and Norman times the King's Gate was an important entrance although it no longer exists; it would have stood where the present St John's Tower now stands.

The newel staircase which connects the upper and lower levels of the keep.

The three levels of St John's Tower still retain the circular stairway which led to the battlements above where a mechanically-balanced platform floor would have tipped a man onto spikes below. Beside this platform is a chute down which boiling oil, molten metal or tar would have been poured onto attackers. Further tunnels branch out of the other side of a small but strong portcullis, built to effectively bar any entrance to them. Although it has never been proved, legend suggests these tunnels led to Guston village, St Radigund's Abbey, Swingate Downs, Northfall Meadow and the Danes. Legend further suggests that Stephen de Pencestre took about 400 men into the castle from Guston when the castle was besieged by Prince Louis of France in 1216. Interestingly, of all these tunnels, when the casemates were being constructed in the eighteenth century the tunnellers were actually working in existing Saxon workings that led from the Pharos to the cliff edge. Passages, shafts and sentry guardrooms hewn from the chalk abound in the western moat area and were either adapted by military engineers or filled in.

Following Henry I's death in 1135 there were conflicts between rivals for the throne of England; his daughter Matilda was supposedly supported by her nephew Stephen who had other ideas and actually seized the throne himself. With a strong force of arms he landed at Dover that same year, but evidently the constable of the castle, John de Fiennes, who was loyal to Henry's daughter, refused to allow his entry to the castle. Undeterred, Stephen took the crown and a year later his wife joined him from France. On 25 October 1154 Stephen died at Dover Priory aged fifty. He was succeeded by the first king of the Plantagenet family, Henry II, one of the most redoubtable and powerful of sovereigns, who was concerned about

Constable's Tower, seen here in 1925.

The keep from Colton's Tower.

Dover being vulnerable to attack from the North European tribes. He not only introduced the system of scutage, whereby the barons surrendered their castle guard duty in exchange for fines payable to the king, but he engaged his own master mason, Maurice the Engineer, who became the first ever recorded master mason. It was he who designed and built the greatest defensive project of all time, replacing the earlier Iron Age settlement, Roman fort, and the outdated Saxon motte and bailey system extensively rebuilt under the Normans and Fulbert de Dover. He supplemented the local hard, durable rag-stone with fine chiselled Caen stone for window and door pillars.

In 1190 Richard I, son and successor of Henry II, assembled his knights and slept in the castle on his way to the Holy Land and the Crusades. Richard's connection with Dover Castle was less than exacting. On the conclusion of the Council of the Realm, held at Canterbury, he rode to Dover from where he set sail for France, eventually to reach the Holy Land on his crusade mission. It is perhaps interesting to record here that during the twelfth and thirteenth centuries the military power of feudalism was crowned by improvements in the design of castle building. Richard's famed Château Gaillard in Normandy and the fortresses of the Crusaders in the east were vastly superior to the mound-and-stockade castles first beheld by the Normans of the conquest era in England. They were eminently superior, even to the 'donjon-keeps', and the new military architecture was a long curtain wall defended by towers placed at intervals along its circuit where it enclosed a single great courtyard (bailey).

Individual English knights continued to go on crusades, although these adventurous energies never became a national tradition as it did in France. It was in the Third Crusade (1190–3) that

King Richard – Coeur de Lion – was acknowledged as the greatest of knights-errant. Indirectly, it was the art of fortification in Asia that was largely imitated in England. Richard I as King of England, was a negligent popular absentee as befitted the character of knight-errant. He had left England, leaving everything in the hands of his brother John. However, Richard had also just appointed Hubert Walter to be Archbishop of Canterbury and Justiciar or Chief Officer of the Crown. It was Hubert who, backed by loyal barons, suppressed the treason of John and purchased Richard's deliverance from an Austrian prison into which his fellow crusaders had thrown him on his return home. Richard rewarded their loyalty by collecting enough money to once more rejoin the Crusades from which he never returned. Hubert Walter, that wise prelate and statesman, not only enforced the King's Peace but also governed England better than Richard would have done.

King John, despite being opposed by the Pope, the cardinals, most of the bishops and a few barons, managed to rebuild or finish much of the castle's defence structures. His success was amply rewarded when, in the hands of that patriotic statesman Hubert de Burgh, he was able to resist the French attack of 1216.

Of the early constables, Hubert de Burgh (1202) stands out as being a capable soldier and organiser. He defended the castle against the French and their allies and not only caused them to raise the siege but went out to sea to meet them and defeated them there. He also strengthened the castle defences by improving the approaches and accommodation within, deepening the moats and ditches and making their sides steeper.

In 1213 the self-appointed King John assembled a large force around Dover, but feared to enter the castle in case his nobles revolted and imprisoned him there. As the king and the baron's parties gained strength in Kent, so the castle changed hands falling on numerous occasions by force of arms or intrigue.

The youngest and only surviving son of Henry II, John, at the age of thirty-two gained the throne of England for which he had been plotting for so long. A copy of the Charter of Liberties, granted by Henry I, had been found in the castle and the barons were determined to enforce its observance. On 20 November 1214, the barons took the oath on the altar of St Edmunds to force from the king an acknowledgement of their rights. They put before John a petition for the renewal of the charter of Henry I. John, after receiving deputies of the barons and hearing their demands, declared that he would never grant them. The barons were now enemies of the Crown and they advanced upon London in May 1215, whereby John had no alternative but to submit. He met the insurgents at Runnymede, a meadow on the banks of the Thames between Windsor and Staines, on 15 June 1215; and four days later signed and sealed the Great Charter of English Liberties, usually known by its Latin designation Magna Carta. The Magna Carta has, ever since, been the fundamental basis of English Liberty, despite John having procured an annulment from Pope Innocent III in September 1215.

John arrived at Dover in July and remained there until September, waiting for his mercenary troops from the Continent. When the barons learned that troops were already stealing into the land, they took up arms and captured Rochester Castle. On hearing this, John left Dover, recaptured Rochester and marched as far as Edinburgh in pursuit of Alexander II of Scotland, who had allied himself with the barons.

Constable's Tower and now the main entrance to Dover Castle sits above the steep moat. (*Author*)

The barons now offered the English throne to the Dauphin of France, Louis VIII, son of Philip Augustus. Dover Castle had been entrusted to Hubert de Burgh, one of the king's most trusted servants. Louis landed at Sandwich on 21 May 1216 and, after seizing Rochester, had entered London where the barons paid homage. Meanwhile, as Louis had already gained control of most of the south-east of England, he attempted to take Dover Castle in July.

The main entrance to the castle at that time was by way of a gateway at the northern side where the Norfolk Tower now stands today. Constructed during John's reign it consisted of two round towers flanking a narrow entrance passage. Beyond this, and reached by a drawbridge, was an outworks on the site of which today is the Redan. Huge oak tree trunks surrounded by a large ditch largely defended the form of this barbican. The castle was well defended by a garrison of 140 knights and their men-at-arms; two of Hubert de Burgh's trusted lieutenants were Gerard de Saltingham and Pierre de Creon. It was necessary for Louis to take the town first while his ships were laid off the coast. Then, after obtaining siege engines from France, and with a formidable force, he began to batter the stout walls.

Hubert de Burgh, with his trusted knights, fought gallantly and destroyed most of the siege equipment until, unable to make any headway, the French commanders were obliged to retreat to safety under a deluge of arrows. Louis was so enraged by this defeat that he swore to take the castle and garrison whatever the cost. He set his miners to undermine the two towers, but only one fell. A second attempt was made upon the North Gate's fallen tower where the French successfully entered the castle through the stone rubble. However, they were eventually pushed back through the breach after which the hole was blocked with timber palisades.

Being in a weak state of health after losing all his baggage, treasures and regalia, including his crown, while crossing the Wash, John developed a fever and was carried to Newark Castle where he died shortly afterwards on 17 October 1216. Word of the king's death quickly reached Dover where Louis asked Hubert de Burgh to surrender the castle. Hubert refused and, adding insult to injury continued to destroy the siege equipment left behind by the retreating French.

To enable Hubert to continue his defence of Dover Castle against the French, Thomas de Sanford gave up over one hundred rings set with emeralds, sapphires, garnets and rubies, to pay for the war. Because taxes had not been collected in areas held by the French, the country could not continue to finance the war by the sale of royal treasures indefinitely. As a result, the regent, William Marshal, took urgent measures to raise money by ordering Falkes de Breauté to give five hundred marks of monies collected in other counties under his control to pay the Dover garrison.

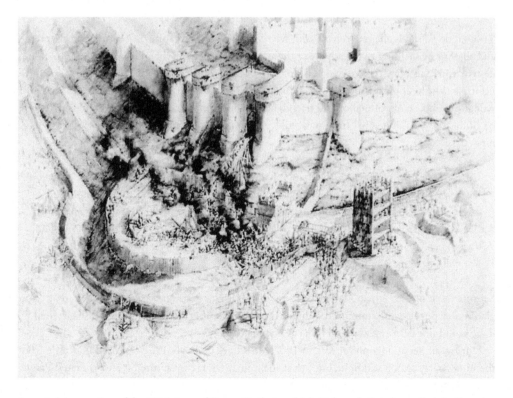

An artist's impression of the 1216 siege of Dover Castle, in which Hubert de Burgh repelled the French.

In January 1217, Louis returned to France for reinforcements and under the threat of ex-communication from the Pope. He returned to England on 23 April 1217 to set about the recapture of the castles he had lost while away, and to resume his siege upon Dover. However, Hubert had reorganised his defences in such a way that Louis was unable to secure a surrender by either force of arms or hunger. Louis sent messengers to Hubert to summon him for a talk. They were the Earl of Salisbury, William Longsword, who had brought with him not only three French nobles, but also Thomas de Burgh, allegedly the brother of Hubert, who had been taken prisoner by Louis at the castle of Norwich. Hubert was accompanied by five of his most skilful crossbowmen who, with bows cocked and arrows fitted, would have killed the messengers at one stroke had there been any sign of treachery. According to the *Histoire des Ducs de Normandie et des Rois d'Angleterre*, Earl Salisbury said, 'Your Lord King is dead and you cannot hold this castle against Louis for long . . . therefore give up the castle and become faithful to Louis who will enrich you with honours and you shall hold a high post among his advisers.' Matthew Paris recorded:

> Louis has sworn that when he has taken possession of this castle by force of arms, all found within it shall be hung without fail. Consult therefore your own safety and honour. You cannot long retain this castle. The power of our Lord Louis increases daily, while that of the king decreases . . . or you will at least perish of hunger . . . therefore without delay or difficulty give up the castle to Louis.

Thomas de Burgh is alleged to have said, 'My dear brother, have compassion on yourself, on me and all of us by yielding to the advice of these nobles; for we will then be freed from impending destruction.' Salisbury then added, 'Listen to my advice Hubert, and obey the will of our Lord Louis, and he will give you as an inheritance, the counties of Norfolk and Suffolk, and you will also be his chief councillor and friend; but if you do not do this your brother Thomas will be hung, and you in a short time will suffer the same punishment.' Hubert is alleged to have replied:

> Earl, wicked traitor that you are, although King John, our Lord and your brother be dead, he has heirs, namely your nephew, whom, although everybody else deserted him, you his uncle ought not to abandon, but ought to be a second father to him; why then base and wicked man that you are, do you talk thus to us? Do not speak another word, because by the lance of God, if you open your mouth to say anything more you shall all be pierced with numbers of arrows, nor will I even spare my own brother.

Salisbury, seeing the crossbowmen were ready to discharge their weapons, retreated at once, glad to escape alive and uninjured. When Louis heard Hubert's reply, although disheartened by it, he could not help applauding Hubert's firmness and resolve.

During the second baron's revolt, in 1263, Sir Roger de Leybourne captured the castle from the king's party after a stiff fight, but lost it again in 1264. He recaptured it and liberated Prince Edward, later Edward I, King of England.

FOUR

WINE, WOMEN & SONG

French attacks on England kept occurring; for example, Dover was burned to the ground in 1295. As we moved into the fourteenth century, French policy decreed that the south-east ports would sustain a lot of damage. This was obviously aimed at shipping and was a policy which would be part of the preparations for invasion of England. Official records reveal the damage to the town, the destruction of houses, the flight of the inhabitants and their reluctance to return, the loss of food and wine and the looting that obviously occurred when the French withdrew.

In 1339 King Edward III wrought havoc upon the French on a vast scale that was greater than all the English towns had suffered. However, because of the French attacks, the castle fortifications, such as the works, arms victuals and garrison, were surveyed and increased.

The Earls of Surrey and of Huntingdon were keepers of the Maritime Lands of Kent. The Earl of Huntingdon was also the constable of Dover Castle, who was charged with victualling and guarding the castle securely. He was in charge of about 100 men, 20 men-at-arms,

40 armed men and 40 archers. The St Martin's Priory was responsible for making the engines of war, armour and the walls for the defence of the town. It was also decreed that all churchmen and laymen were to live as close to the sea as was possible. In no instances were archers to be taken from the maritime lands.

A couple of local burgesses were entrusted with being 'Keepers of the Maritime Lands', a sort of Home Guard, who were entrusted with extensive powers for the defence of their own area. A typical statement of their duties says:

> To guard the coast of Dover and the whole of the maritime land of the county.
> To resist invaders whether they come by sea or land.
> To take steps necessary for the safety of the realm.
> To make suitable appointments.
> To require that, after due warning, the sheriff shall parade the posse before them.

In 1364 Edward III stayed at the castle and issued new regulations regarding the Cinque Ports Fleet, which was then of considerable proportions.

Between 1415 and 1450 there was a great massing of men at Dover Castle for the wars in France and Belgium. The English Channel was in constant turmoil, piracy was rampant and the local seamen were not particularly unblemished.

Constable's Garden with St Mary's Tower on the right.

In 1519 the castle was visited by King Henry VIII who assembled his retinue there before crossing to France for the 'Field of the Cloth of Gold'.

Then, in 1522 Henry VIII waited in Dover Castle to receive the Emperor Charles V. The housing capacity must have been considerably strained to accommodate the assembled noblemen and church dignitaries. The king seemed to have great regard for Dover, as he had at different times no less than three of his recognised wives there, and made home there on several occasions when great feasting and tournaments took place.

Between 1540 and 1560 many important structural alterations took place; most of the outer curtain wall was repaired and strengthened, largely as the introduction of gunpowder required new defensive positions to be made. During that time (1555) Queen Mary visited the castle.

Looking along the curtain wall with Peverell's Tower on the right, we get a remarkable view of the defence structure leading to the harbour.

Cast in bronze, 'Queen Elizabeth's Pocket Pistol' stood unprotected for years and only recently was it moved under cover to aid its preservation.

In 1573 Queen Elizabeth I visited the castle when the ceremonial pomp surpassed anything that had gone on before. She was so impressed with it that she extended her stay to a week and was encouraged to make several grants from the exchequer to improve the castle and harbour. She again visited the castle for a short stay and it was on that occasion she had mounted in the castle grounds the Long Gun, later known as 'Queen Elizabeth's Pocket Pistol'. Made of brass and cast in Utrecht, Holland, in 1544, the 24ft long gun was originally intended as a present for Henry VIII from the Emperor Charles V, but as they had fallen out of favour with each other the presentation never took place. When Elizabeth entered into an alliance with Holland, the gun was presented to her instead. Interestingly, the gun carriage upon which it now rests was made by the order of the Duke of Wellington, and is built from cannon brought back from the battlefields of Waterloo. The inscription on it is in Dutch and reads, 'Brech Scuet Al Mver Ende Wal, Bin Ich Geheten, Dver Bergh En Dal Boest Minen Bal, Van Mi Gemesten.' The translation reads, 'To break surely earthwork and wall am I made through hill and vale goes my ball by me propelled.'

In 1647 when Royalist troops were away with King Charles I, the Dover garrison consisted of less than twenty men. Local people took advantage of this and captured it for Cromwell, who immediately sent sufficient Parliamentary troops to hold the fortress. Then, in 1648 Kentish Royalists attacked the castle but were defeated.

In 1660 Charles II landed at Dover but did not stay at the castle until some years later when he made a journey through Kent on one of his many pleasure trips.

Between 1704 and 1707 Queen Anne visited the castle and made several grants for improvements, one being the roof over the annexe to the keep. Several barrack rooms were also built to house infantry stationed there.

FIVE

AN ONEROUS TASK

In 1750 the castle defences underwent many rapid changes. Early Saxon towers, Norman walls and some Tudor buildings were demolished without any recourse to their subsequent historical value. They were to make way for new roads and important gun positions. The military architects paid no regard to sentiment, and no attempt was made to preserve for future generations the landmarks of a nation's history. Today the archaeologists might say that some demolition was quite unnecessary and showed little regard for anything of importance.

In 1774 and forty-odd years thence, Dover Castle became a great military centre where troops were stationed, although the majority were either billeted in alehouses, livery stables or inns. Many were encamped in tents outside the castle boundary walls. As the fortunes of war varied so the garrison grew or shrunk. Sometimes the castle was never in possession of a complete unit and on those few occasions the castle possessed one or two infirm or elderly gunners.

In 1795 the castle was thoroughly surveyed and its defences modernised so that when Napoleon's army was assembled at Boulogne in 1801, the commander at the castle possessed an almost impregnable fortress. The country, and especially Dover, was galvanised into military activity by the threat of Napoleon Bonaparte and his threatened invasion. The castellated towers of the inner ward, built originally by Henry II, were levelled off and filled with rubble to make gun platforms. Numerous cannon emplacements were also built, and the castle defences put in some sort of order for the invasion that never came.

It was during the Napoleonic Wars, between 1793 and 1815, when Royal Engineer miners began burrowing into the chalk cliff on which 'The Key of England' majestically sits.

Simultaneous to the addition of barracks, gun emplacements, moats and the paraphernalia of war at the castle, similar construction was going on to the west of Dover, on the Western Heights. At the castle seven tunnels, later called casemates, were being driven inwards from the cliff face within the castle boundary. The chalk strata, a soft white limestone deposit, the origins of which date back about 100 million years, is easy to work and relatively safe to excavate. It is a cleaner, much less sticky material than, say, clay, and infinitely less dangerous than sand, a fact not lost on military engineers. The miners began their onerous task of hand-digging these tunnels from the south-east cliff face in about 1797.

Two groups of three parallel tunnels ran in from the cliff face, substantial in size and brick-lined, the whole concept providing an unusual form of underground barracks, the first

A sentry's platform, spy hole and light shaft.

A Napoleonic barrack room.

of its kind in Britain. At the seaward end of the tunnels there were going to be installed the guns and at the inward end of each tunnel, vertical ventilation shafts were cut to afford a draught of air to disperse gun smoke. Access to these tunnels was served by a smaller, unlined communication passage, which linked each of them at the rear. Near the southern or seaward end of the easternmost tunnel, later to become the Admiralty Casemate in the Second World War, a second communication passage was cut behind the cliff face linking the eastern group to an open area in front of the three western tunnels, known as the terrace. At the terrace's most western end, a brick-lined tunnel gradually sloped upwards to the main castle level, which was the recognised route through which heavy guns and associated equipment could be moved into the casemates. By the time construction of these tunnels was finished in about 1810, however, the threat of invasion had largely diminished, and no existing record suggests the guns were ever mounted in each casemate during the remainder of the Napoleonic Wars. We do know, however, the tunnels and passages were kept open and maintained after Napoleon's defeat at Waterloo, so that when the First World War broke out in 1914, they were used for less exciting storage purposes and the more exacting Dover Patrol's Port War Signal Station, situated above on the cliff face.

At the end of the Napoleonic Wars in about 1815 the poor of England were insufficiently protected from poverty; as men were discharged from their regiments and the navy they, in turn, became a burden upon the populace. It was not surprising, therefore, that smuggling, which had thrived since the early thirteenth century when wool was the main export to the Continent, should suddenly take a leap in popularity. The counties of Kent and Sussex, both

One of several tunnels crudely finished beneath Dover Castle and eventually used as a communication passageway during the Second World War.
(English Heritage)

close to the Continent and the shortest route through which smuggling had been achieved for many centuries, was always in the forefront of any clandestine operation.

The Revenue Service was losing its grip by the eighteenth century. Efforts to eradicate the tremendous loss of revenue were redoubled in 1817, when the admiralty decided to accept the advice of a Captain William Joseph McCulloch, R.N. His proposal was to set up blockade stations at strategic intervals along the coasts of Kent and Sussex, between which foot patrols of seamen under the command of a lieutenant were implemented. There ensued some frightening battles between smugglers and revenue men.

In 1817 Captain McCulloch had set up his headquarters in the now disused casemates. Castles were considerably less important as a means of defence by then and mobile armies and their commanders just used them as a fortress-base in which to garrison troops. Between the casemates and the foreshore a new path was cut into the cliff face, by which means the revenue men could quickly reach the beach below.

In the event Captain McCulloch not only proposed the new blockade system but also organised a permanent beach cordon of armed ex-naval men known as 'Sentinels'.

Within five years his eighty or so men had grown to over 3,000 naval officers and men. They came under a strict naval discipline but, although armed with cutlasses, pistols and rifles, were usually no match for the armed smuggling gangs. By the nineteenth century the Customs Board estimated that smuggling had increased alarmingly with about 4½ tons of tea arriving daily. Captain McCulloch's secure base in the casemates was an ideal observation point. It was also ideal for another purpose. McCulloch received a letter of complaint from the Guardian of the Poor at Dover in March 1822. It read, 'Very loose and disorderly women are filling different buildings occupied by the Blockade men, some of whom were pregnant.' It was later estimated that more than twenty-two women were living there.

The last attack on the Kent blockade line was made near the casemate station on 31 January 1831, when twenty or so smugglers managed to overcome a couple of sentinels. As was often the case, the smugglers got clean away with their contraband, leaving behind on the beach just one bale of silk.

The Coast Artillery by 1899 had evolved into the Garrison Artillery and was a vast step forward providing a proper chain of command. When war broke out in 1914 Dover possessed only two RGA Companies, a further reduction from six in 1860. While these two companies serving Dover had been reduced, their available weapons had increased. By 1880 it was realised

Some nineteenth-century graffiti cut into the chalk walls beneath Dover Castle left by the Royal Garrison Artillery. *(English Heritage)*

the casemate system was out of date. For one thing it was conspicuous and could be seen from any anchored warship; for another reason the smoke, which after only a few rounds had been fired, seriously impeded the gunners and restricted their field of fire. A new 'en barbette' – an earthen terrace behind a rampart and terrace, the latter being the gun position – was implemented by 1914. By then the port of Dover consisted of Nos 40 and 46 Coy RGA and No. 1 Coy Kent RGA, the latter a territorial force.

The carnage of the First World War had no impact on the castle for it never featured in any defence measures other than the Dover Patrol's Port War Signal Station within the grounds. The Royal Garrison Artillery had had their offices at the castle since Napoleonic times but in 1914 moved to Victoria Park. Also, officers and crew, survivors of the German submarine *U8*, scuttled by destroyers of the Dover Patrol on 4 March 1915, were lodged in the castle.

When, on Sunday 19 March 1916, a German seaplane dropped bombs in the harbour and at Northfall Meadow near the castle, one bomb exploded on a hut occupied by members of the 5th Battalion Royal Fusiliers, killing four men and injuring eleven others. Soon afterwards, another German seaplane arrived dropping bombs on the castle, but only seemed to destroy the confidence placed in the anti-aircraft defences at Dover; the slow-moving targets were easy ones to hit by the meagre defences, but they never hit anything. As a result of comments made in parliament in 1916, referring to the defenceless state of Dover against air raids, anti-aircraft guns were mounted in the castle. A Hotchkiss six-pounder quick-firing pom-pom was erected on the corner of the old Roman earthworks near the Pharos. Searchlights were placed at the Drop Redoubt, Western Heights, on the castle keep and at Langdon Battery, where a twelve-pounder anti-aircraft gun was also installed.

Contrary to popular belief a hospital was never built in the castle tunnels during the First World War period. The 1,215,886 hospital cases landed at Dover by the hospital ships from France were put immediately onto ambulance trains, which carried them further inland.

SIX

'FUSE ALL WARHEADS'

The requisition of the castle in the Second World War produced a formula of external and internal changes due to unavoidable forces. Despite the high costs and frequent inconvenience of tunnelling, the fortress developed prestige and influence. The requisition in 1939 broke the thread of a castle being untended and largely unoccupied, its empty rooms symbolic of the substantial country houses on landed estates. The causes of destruction of the many medieval buildings within its boundary walls during the late eighteenth century are,

This 1932 picture shows the Black Watch Regiment on parade at Dover Castle. The Victoria barracks, seen on the right, was demolished in the 1970s.

perhaps, too painfully obvious. They were in the way and so today rest in folk memory only, but neither Napoleon, the Kaiser or Hitler ever destroyed Dover's historic buildings as were done-away-with by eighteenth-century engineers.

It was during the Second World War, with the enemy only 21 miles away, that the underground Napoleonic complex really came into its own. Vice-Admiral Ramsay and his naval staff moved in to occupy the eastern casemate in 1939 where he created his first operations room. A telegraphist serving with Vice-Admiral Ramsay's staff, who arrived just one week before the war actually started, recalled receiving a signal from the Admiralty on 3 September 1939 to 'fuse all warheads – prepare for war.'

The first enemy Charles Seyd remembers was the hordes of bats and rats that lived in the tunnels and passages, the latter he said, being 'big enough to jump up and reach the door handles.'

It was from the casemate in the Second World War, in what would become famously known as the Admiralty Casemate, nearly 200ft below ground level, that Vice-Admiral Bertram Ramsay, Flag Officer Dover, secretly masterminded the evacuation of over 300,000 British and Allied troops from the beaches of Dunkirk.

After the Dunkirk evacuation the coastal artillery moved in to the casemates from Fort Burgoyne too and in 1941, over 4,000 gunners were controlled from this point. They were given a small room known as the 'Movements Room' where they plotted the positions of not only enemy shipping, but also our own ships to avoid mistakenly sinking them.

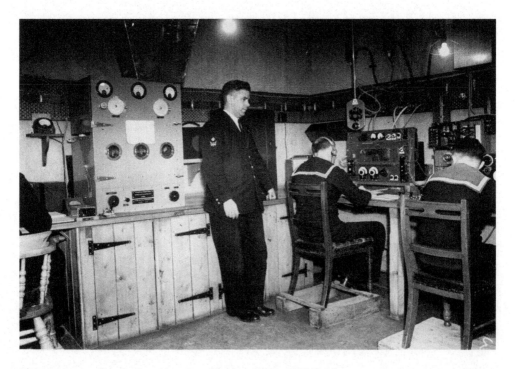

This picture was taken in the early years of the Second World War of the casemate wireless room at Dover Castle. *(Imperial War Museum)*

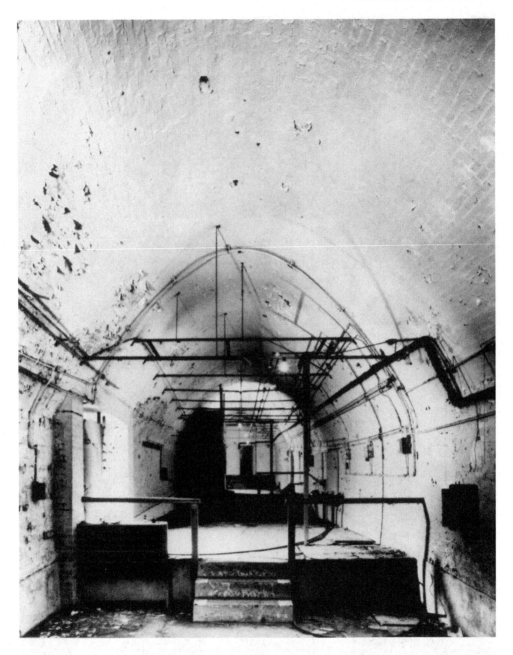

One of several brick-lined tunnels first cut into chalk beneath Dover Castle during the Napoleonic period and later used in the Second World War as a telecommunications facility. *(English Heritage)*

This posed picture, taken by Lt Tanner in 1941 in one of several newly constructed tunnels beneath Dover Castle, depicts the liaison of Army, Navy and RAF personnel in a combined operations mode. *(Imperial War Museum)*

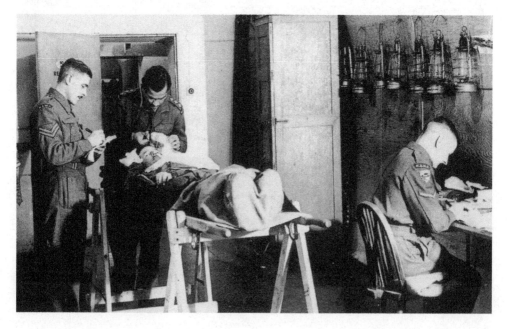

This posed picture, taken by Lt Tanner in about 1942, shows a minor operation being performed in the ANNEXE level of Dover Castle.

Based at the Royal Engineers' supply depot, Canterbury, Sergeant Thomas Groves was responsible for supplying corrugated sheet steel and its upright supports to various tunnelling companies working in South-East Command. In the following year, promoted to Sergeant-Major, he was on permanent attachment to Dover Castle, arranging supplies directly to detachments of the Nos 171, 172 and 173 Tunnelling Companies, Royal Engineers, who were busy cutting through chalk immediately above the original Napoleonic casemates. This new section became known as ANNEXE and was to house a dressing station, dormitories, kitchens and messing facilities, where later the dressing station was extended to a 500-bed hospital with two operating theatres. A detachment of No. 172 Tunnelling Company had

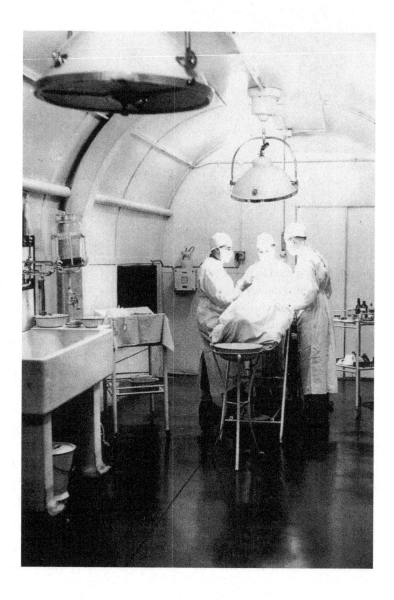

This posed picture, again captured by Lt Tanner in about 1942, also depicts the operating theatre at ANNEXE level.

Working at the chalk face, sappers cut only enough area to accommodate the steel support structures to maintain safety. The lightweight Holman pick was an ideal tool for cutting into chalk and – undeniably – a body-building exercise too. *(Imperial War Museum)*

recently been shifted from Gibraltar where they had been engaged cutting through solid rock. Most were dressed in only a woollen cap, denim trousers and heavy, steel-capped boots, and they said cutting through chalk was a piece of cake. Lt-Col Swale, Staff Captain to No. 219 Infantry Brigade, especially remembered the presence of so many 'unexpected female talent', not least, because the WRNS of Admiral Ramsay's staff were so punctilious in their salutes to officers whenever they passed or met. Ramsay's staff had a system of 'Officer Only' delivering messages by WRN officers. The rule was that these officers could go singly in the tunnels before 1900 hrs but thereafter there had to be two of them. 'Presumably,' Lt-Col Swale said, 'the Admiralty was unaware that the tunnels were well underground and unaffected by daylight.' Jean Aitchison, a WRN with the meteorological office – the third back from the Admiral's balcony – usually took messages from the Lamson vacuum tube system, but this often broke down, resulting in her going down into the bowels of the castle to collect them from the teleprinter room, where the WRN operators understood the Creed relays and the Baud's system of tolerance on the machines. The signal distribution office received restricted and confidential messages by teleprinter, W/T (Morse), Aldis Lamp and telephone, and most needed decoding.

During the many shelling alerts, the staff had to remain 'on station' and were only allowed to go as far as the canteen and sleeping quarters situated in the old casemate tunnels. Everyone found the conditions in the tunnels – cold, damp, dark and poorly ventilated – dreary and they

Shooting chalk spoil through the cliff face was a tiresome job that required skill and certain awareness of safety so that neither the truck nor you would disappear over the edge. *(Imperial War Museum)*

were the reasons for many bronchial discomforts of one kind or another. Lt-Col Swale recalled his own little office, which had inadequate strip lighting and a defective two-bar electric fire with worn-out elements that had to be supplemented by paper clips.

Castle defence in 1940, should there have been an invasion, was both bizarre and medieval in concept. Private Pearce with the 15th Battalion, Queen's Royal Regiment, recalled the chalk passages were lined with obsolete 40lb RAF bombs. Elsewhere were stored a number of wooden frames approximately 12ft long, supported on legs which were about 18in high. These frames consisted of two solid wooden planks about 6in wide, and they were fixed to the legs to form a 'V'-shaped channel, rather like a narrow trough. In the event of an invasion, they would be strategically placed outside and along the cliff top in front of the officers' mess building, overlooking the houses below at East Cliff. The intention was to place the bombs in the 'V' troughs and direct them over the cliff edge towards the invaders at the foot of the cliff.

Interceptions, battles and skirmishes between a variety of German warships, Royal Navy Motor Torpedo Boats (MTBs) and Motor Gun Boats (MGBs), coupled with enemy long-range artillery activity shelling shore installations and shipping in the Dover Strait, was monitored by staff working a three-shift system below ground at the castle. Information received, both day and night, from coastal observation posts, RAF reconnaissance pilots, warships, radar stations and every conceivable intelligence network was both exciting and exacting. However, as the war effort expanded, so the tunnels became crammed with communication equipment and the people to use it.

Re-installed by English Heritage beneath Dover Castle is the repeater equipment used during the Second World War. *(English Heritage)*

Ever mindful of the putty-like chalk layers between layers of flint, sappers cut into the tunnel face with a Holman pick beneath Dover Castle in 1942. *(Imperial War Museum)*

A decision was taken in early 1941 to extend the tunnels slightly above and to the rear of the eastern Admiralty Casemate. Additional tunnellers were brought in to excavate a new level, which was intended to accommodate a combined headquarters complex called BASTION. It was an ambitious plan consisting of an upper grid-pattern floor cut just behind and to the rear of the old Napoleonic casemates. It was intended, not only to ease pressure of space, but as an important second available HQ should the operations centre outside Portsmouth be put out of action. To minimise disturbance of the existing naval and army facilities, a working tunnel was begun from the East Moat area. At the same time a separate tunnel was also started at the rear of the casemate level, running almost parallel with the rear communication tunnel at the base of the spiral stairway, intending to link the new complex to the casemates.

More than 50 per cent had been completed when severe subsidence occurred and, after consultation, the whole of BASTION was abandoned immediately. The only proper entrance before it was abandoned had been through the construction tunnel which was intended as an air vent passage and came out into the East Moat area through which all the chalk spoil was removed. To prevent further subsidence, this tunnel entrance was cleared and the corrugated sheet steel linings removed, allowing BASTION to be back-filled with rubble then finally being cemented over before the moat wall was rebuilt. An emergency flight of stairs at the back of the complex had already been cut through to within a few feet of the surface within the castle grounds when the work was suddenly stopped. Several millions of cubic feet of chalk spoil had to be disposed of and this became the subject of a report signed by the Superintending Engineer on 4 March 1942, which stated 'considerable difficulties in "Red Herring" planning due to spoil exposure ... ensure prompt action following "O" date completion ... to study long term camouflage policy.' Most of the spoil, if not all of it, was being tipped into the sea just off of the eastern arm of the harbour and was revealed on RAF reconnaissance photographs.

Particularly recognisable by his wristwatch, Jack Tincombe of 693 Artisan Works Company, Royal Engineers, is seen levelling a paving slab in one of the newly constructed tunnels beneath Dover Castle in 1941. (Imperial War Museum)

On completion of the DUMPY combined services HQ beneath Dover Castle, No. 1 Section 639 Artisan Works Company, Royal Engineers, pose for this photograph in October 1943. *(L.A. Turner, RE)*

In late 1942 cutting recommenced at a lower level beneath the casemates, forming an area of tunnels, passages and rooms that, by 1943, became known as DUMPY. The chalk strata beneath the castle was easily cut into by the Holman pneumatic picks that were connected by airlines to the compressed air generator units situated outside in the moat area. The DUMPY complex of tunnels was in fact extended outwards from a small former Napoleonic magazine reached through an old lift shaft. Occasional heavy rainfall would often penetrate through the chalk strata and was still a problem even after the corrugated sheet steel linings were erected by sappers of No. 693 Artisan Works Company, Royal Engineers, allowing any seepage to be directed round them and into the extensive, and sometimes complicated, main drainage system.

The DUMPY complex was eventually fitted out with everything to convert it into a fully equipped operational headquarters for the joint services. Similar in every respect to the way the BASTION complex had been planned, a Ruston & Hornsby power generator back-up system was installed along with an up-to-date air conditioning system, installed by G.N. Haden of Trowbridge, allowing for dormitories, offices and other facilities. Communication between the various offices was provided by the efficient, although dated, Lamson vacuum tube system, whereby messages were quickly transferred in cylindrical carriers propelled by compressed air through 3in diameter tubes.

Finished tunnels, passages, rooms and cubicles would eventually have installed the telephone switchboards, teleprinters, wireless receivers, radar sets, plotting boards and maps which were moved down from the original casemates. In the event, this did not happen as most of the equipment installed was new and a duplication of paraphernalia already in use in the above casemates. There were, however, grumbles of resistance by female clerks – WRNS, ATS and WAAFs – who perhaps even had had a glimmer of some new vision of Utopia in the bowels of the castle. The quality of their surroundings was never seen as an indulgence as the planned description of the new scheme was of a large penetration of a maze of tunnels and passages and vaults. Not only were the female clerks reluctant to move where, as before, they were to continue to decode cipher messages and move symbols over the plotting tables, but their male colleagues were equally disillusioned.

A letter to South Eastern Command, dated 23 February 1942, from GHQ Home Forces, stated, 'With regard to the Dover project . . . There is a considerable amount of tunnelled accommodation in the castle other than that in the actual casemates.' The following extract from a letter dated 1 March 1942, states, 'The additional tunnelled accommodation at Dover is required so that 90 ATS on the staff of CCCA, and Garrison Command, Dover, may live underground under conditions of prolonged siege and constant bombing attacks to which this fortress may well be subjected.' The next paragraph says, 'It is pointed out that, even if the rest of Dover should be overrun by the enemy, the castle itself is a very strong defended locality which is intended to hold out independently and must therefore be self-contained.'

Cpl Elizabeth Amery at work in the plotting room. (Imperial War Museum)

One of the brick-lined casemates used by the Royal Navy beneath Dover Castle during the Second World War. This cubicle was adjacent to the admiral's cabin, the window of which can be seen beyond the upper skylight. *(Imperial War Museum)*

Paragraph 5 states, 'Apart from the casemates, all of which are fully occupied, there are certain passages on the north side, but these are unsuitable for the following reasons: -

They are not deep enough to give adequate protection.

They would involve a ten-minute walk from the casemates across open ground.

They are merely passages and would require substantial alterations to make them habitable.

Paragraph 7 states, 'For similar reasons it is recommended that VA Dover's proposals for tunnelled accommodation for his WRNs also be approved so that the two tasks can be carried out at the same time.'

Dated 26 June and signed by Major Mackenzie, the following is revealed:

'E' says that some of No. 172 Tunnelling Coy may be available to start new work by 15 July. Before going any further, however, they require confirmation of the following points:

That the project at Dover is the construction of a Combined HQ similar to that at Fort Southwick.
That the present occupants of the existing underground accommodation at Dover (i.e. VA Dover, Garrison Commander and CCCA) will continue to occupy their present scale of accommodation.

Decisions were also required on the following points:

(a) If the present occupants at Dover are to remain does the Combined HQ have to be close to them, i.e. under the castle, or could it be on the other side of the town under the Western Heights?

(b) Is above-ground accommodation required as well as underground?

It was not until October 1942, that any confirmation was sought to provide two subsidiary tunnelled dugouts required for wireless transmitter stations located about a mile from the castle, each of which were to be about 100ft by about 10ft, with two adits of about 200ft. The completion date for installation of power supplies to these two transmitter stations, one at Langdon Hole and another at the Danes, was required by the same date as the main complex of tunnels under the castle. The OC of No. 172 Tunnelling Coy estimated that excavation of each new tunnel would take from six to eight weeks to complete. He said that he could not spare any men from the main tunnel complex (DUMPY) if it was to be completed any earlier. He further suggested that if the whole project was put back a month he would need about sixty extra tunnellers from about 1 November for two months.

It was not until December 1942 that the gas proofing of the Dover casemates was brought up for discussion, but it was decided not to proceed with this proposal. What had upset everyone was that a new tunnel entrance was required, because most of the post office equipment already installed was blocking the entrance to cubicles and passages. While removal of the equipment was strongly suggested, everyone knew it would prove a disastrous undertaking as it was in constant use. The equipment remained in situ until a new tunnel was especially cut through, joining two casemates.

Tunnelling personnel largely consisted of volunteers, drawn from various arms of the services, including RE training battalions. The majority came from Northumberland, Durham, Wales and Scotland. They were a tough, undisciplined bunch, and were said to be an NCO's nightmare. The tunnels reverberated to the unending rattle of pneumatic drills and the drone of air compressors. Even that incessant din was eclipsed by the heroic clamour of conveyor belts shifting hundreds of cubic feet of chalk away from the immediate tunnel face.

The installation of artillery pieces in the Dover area when the threat of invasion was imminent in 1940, had largely depended on 6in guns facing seawards, under the command of No. 519 Coast Artillery, RA, while larger pieces, such as the 8in land guns at Lydden Spout, came under No. 520 Coast Artillery, RA. Inadequate range of both these guns to bracket enemy shipping sailing near the French coast a year later, meant that larger calibre guns were needed. Churchill was quick to insist that 15in guns should be installed, with the result that two of them – later named 'Jane' and 'Clem' – were placed at Wanstone Farm, with four 9.2in guns installed at South Foreland under No. 540 Coast Artillery, RA. Additionally, the Royal Marine Siege Regiment became responsible for two 14in guns – named 'Winnie' and 'Pooh' – located on the St Margaret's golf course, east of Dover. At Guston, a further three 13.5in railway-mounted guns named 'Sceneshifter', 'Piecemaker' and 'Gladiator' were also installed. Prime Minister Winston Churchill visited the castle on 24 January 1941 especially to see the installation of his 'big guns' at Wanstone Farm, but was furious to learn that their completion was delayed by the lack of suitable gun mountings and deficiencies of ammunition, fuses and charges.

While the coastal artillery lacked the firepower to reach enemy shipping, the Dover-based Coastal Force, consisting of MTBs and MGBs, enthusiastically got involved with attacking these targets on any pretence. Their first successful torpedo attack was made just before midnight on 8 September, 1941, when two 3,000-ton German merchant ships, escorted by armed trawlers, were seen on coastal radar leaving Boulogne harbour, attempting to pass through the Dover Strait. Naval staff in the casemates were first alerted when a cipher message dropped into the basket from the Lamson system. Within minutes the Coastal Force was signalled to engage the enemy. On a calm, moonlit night they closed in unseen and delivered their torpedoes with devastating accuracy. They were in action again in November when they sank a 5,000-ton German merchant ship in a furious engagement, during which one MGB was seriously damaged by return fire. It lay off Cap Gris-Nez with its radio system inoperative, until spotted by a Spitfire pilot who raised the alarm.

Coastal Force, and more especially the naval staff at Dover Castle, were disgusted with the lack of initiative on 12 February 1942. Thick fog blanketed the Dover Strait when, under cover of darkness, the German battle cruisers *Scharnhorst* and *Gneisenau*, together with the heavy cruiser *Prinz Eugen*, sailed out of Brest harbour. At dawn, screened by destroyers and E-boats with Messerschmitt fighter cover, they steamed east in poor visibility. Because Fairlight radar, on the Sussex coast, was out of action, a Spitfire pilot only later confirmed the position of

General Sir John Dill, Chief of the Imperial General Staff, and Vice-Admiral Sir Bertram Ramsay, Flag Office Dover, accompany the Prime Minister Winston Churchill on his visit to the Port War Signal Station above Dover Castle in June 1941. *(Imperial War Museum)*

Winston Churchill in the observation post from which he witnessed an air battle. The mayor of Dover is seen in the foreground. *(Imperial War Museum)*

the battleships as they entered the narrowest part of the Dover Strait off Boulogne. Led by Lt–Cdr Pumphrey, MTBs set course to intercept, but hampered by a dense smoke screen laid around the warships, Pumphrey's torpedoes never had a chance of hitting their targets. He had reluctantly retired by the time Brigadier Raw decided to engage with his 9.2in South Foreland battery. With visibility down to about 5 miles, the targets were at extreme range and could not be seen with the naked eye. The guns opened fire at approximately 30,000yds range for about fifteen minutes until the warships passed completely out of range. Raw was annoyed that his 15in guns at Wanstone were still being installed and later made the comment that 'had they been ready there is little doubt considerable damage would have been inflicted.' His criticism was a valid point, proved beyond doubt, when later, several vessels were successfully bracketed and were either damaged or sunk by the 15in guns.

Taken in October 1942, this photograph shows Field Marshal Jan Smuts with Winston Churchill on the terrace at Dover Castle looking over the harbour. A Lewis machine gun is mounted beside the range-finder. *(Imperial War Museum)*

Winston Churchill visited the castle not only in 1940 and 1941, but also in October 1942, when he became fascinated with his 'big guns', now able to fire at enemy shipping. He was concerned by the devastation caused to civilian property when the German big guns fired on Dover in retaliation. On that occasion the South African Boer War veteran and confidant of the prime minister, Field Marshal Jan Christian Smuts, the Turkish Ambassador Mr Morganthau and William Averell Harriman, the US Ambassador, accompanied him. Vice-Admiral H.D. Pridham-Wippell was now Flag Officer Dover. By then Ramsay had left for other duties and would later be nominated Commander-in-Chief, Naval Forces, prior to Operation Overlord, the Allied invasion of France on 6 June 1944.

Churchill showed great interest in the lower level DUMPY combined services complex, nearing completion, and which was to house the supplementary Naval, Army and RAF

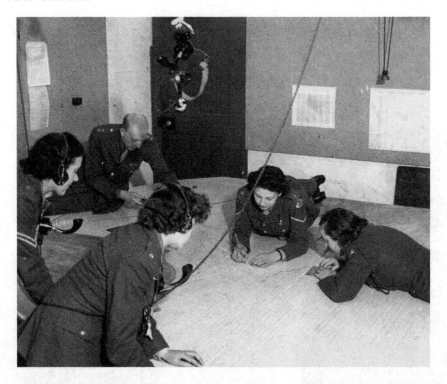

ATS girls busy plotting enemy ship movements in the English Channel.
(Imperial War Museum)

Winston Churchill in steel helmet during an air battle which took place during his visit.
(Imperial War Museum)

Winston Churchill with Vice-Admiral Ramsay inspecting maps.

units, in addition to the proven casemate system still active above. He was, however, amused to discover the previous Flag Officer Dover had refused to vacate his office because, through his window in the casemate, he could observe the 'goings on' outside. Rosemary Keyes (Lord Keyes's Niece) served as a WRN cipher officer and remembers the rabbit warren of dark, dreary, damp and airless passages and rooms. 'We worked all day in electric light and only saw daylight when we went to the "heads" to spend a penny. This was a small room which contained a noisome "thunderbox", but a beautiful view over Dover Harbour, seen through a small window cut into the cliff face, but only if you stood on the lavatory seat.'

The multifarious telephone cables which were eventually connected with DUMPY came from coastal gun sites, anti-aircraft sites, brigade headquarters, fortress plotting rooms, gun plotting rooms, airfields and air sea rescue, not to mention the naval operations. It was a source of wonder to the uninitiated how the telephone engineers knew which wire was which when repairs were needed. Even more disconcerting was that the whole gamut tended to confuse the

Winston Churchill looking through reports. With him is Vice-Admiral Ramsay.

most intelligent of staff when no one was quite sure who was who, who worked where and what their particular job was. Security became a nightmare. Military Police of all three services were not only at the entrance to the castle, but also at the entrance to the tunnels. Armed guards were on sentry duties around the whole castle perimeter. 'No pass, no entry' was a strict order and woe betide anyone caught without their pass.

The coastal plotting tables, anti-aircraft plotting tables, air sea rescue plotting tables, maps and charts in the plotting rooms only made sense to those WRNS, ATS and WAAFs working on them in a confined space, lit only by the occasional bulk-head light fitting or an isolated bulb hanging from conduit in the casemates. When the lower level DUMPY was completed, fluorescent lighting was introduced. When the RAF liaison team arrived in 1943, and because of the ceiling height restriction, they had insisted their plotting table should be sunk at floor level, overlooked by a high, curved, perspex-fronted balcony from which controllers looked down, similar in every respect to the efficient fighter airfield systems then in use.

Les Turner of the No. 693 Artisan Works Company, RE, is identified on the left in this photograph taken by an official photographer at Dover Castle in 1942. The steps lead to DUMPY. *(Imperial War Museum)*

An office in the tunnels beneath Dover Castle.

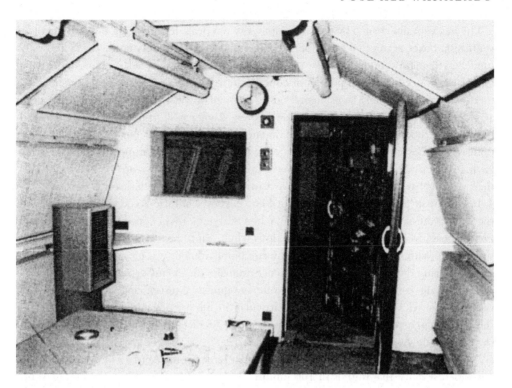

The BBC room at DUMPY level.

A passage leading to DUMPY level

The incessant din created by the air compressors and drills, reverberating through the metal ventilation boxes, permeated every room, cubicle and passage throughout the casemates, as the tunnellers frantically cut through new chalk in an effort to finish their task on time. In the event, cipher clerks needed special powers of concentration to make sense out of umpteen coded messages, especially when a large enemy convoy was seen on radar leaving Boulogne harbour on 12 March 1943. It gave an excuse for Coastal Force – laying at 'short notice' in the Ferry Dock – to quickly shoot through the Eastern Arm entrance in Dover's harbour in hot pursuit. Both flotillas of MTBs and MGBs came under ferocious gunfire from escorting armed trawlers and, having successfully damaged one vessel and left another listing, they returned to Dover to lick their wounds, having sustained considerable damage and casualties in the action.

It was not all 'plain sailing' for the Coastal Force. They sent furious coded radio messages to the naval plotting room on 28 June 1943, when a large German convoy was spotted off the French coast. MTBs scattered in all directions when Wanstone's 15in guns 'Jane' and 'Clem' opened fire without prior warning. The precise bombardment was preceded by the Fan Bay 6in guns firing their usual 'flash-fire' sequence, to make the enemy vessels alter course into a predictable zig-zag pattern, allowing the plotters to quickly estimate range and course of each individual vessel. Unfortunately, in this particular 56-minute engagement when about fifty shells had been expended, only one hit was recorded. Predictably, within 15 minutes, German shells rained down on the town and the gun batteries.

When a large German convoy was seen on radar screens on 5 April 1943, Wanstone's 15in guns used seventy-five rounds in 106 minutes. Thirteen hits were observed before South Foreland joined in the action. Their logbook records one 1,000-ton vessel sunk and another severely damaged. When two German destroyers were plotted on radar near Dunkirk on 5 July 1943, it gave the Wanstone and South Foreland batteries some target practice lasting fifty-two minutes. Between them they fired sixty shells at a range of 32,000yds, but when the MTBs joined in unannounced, the firing ceased. Vital and precise information of the MTBs' whereabouts was imperative and liaison between the naval and artillery-plotting rooms became a crucial factor.

The overall success of the 'big guns' on 4 September 1943 was an example of the precise plotting required when German ships were bracketed off Calais, sinking one and setting fire to another. The Fan Bay 6in guns fired their usual 'flash-fire' sequence before the bigger guns opened fire. Further successes came when, just after midnight on 4 October 1943, a forty-minute bombardment sent thirty-five 15in shells and fifty-six 9.2in shells bracketing a German convoy off Cap Gris-Nez. One vessel was sunk while two others were so severely damaged they were observed beaching. On 25 October, a 104-minute bombardment of enemy ships off Calais resulted in one large vessel being sunk after about eighty shells fell among them. The townspeople were not amused when German long-range artillery commenced shelling the town, demolishing several houses in the process.

When two enemy destroyers were bracketed while steaming up the Channel on 3 November 1943, the cipher messages were being distributed at top speed, but made all the more difficult when cipher officers had to avoid treading on sleeping bodies. Tired staff just lay on the floor and went to sleep, having worked non-stop without a break. A WRN teleprinter operator remembered the 'wonderful whiff of fresh air after surfacing from night duty even if it was raining. The atmosphere below ground could be pretty foul, even though salty air was being pumped through to the lower levels. And then there was the time the Lamson vacuum tube system broke down, which always seemed to occur at a crucial moment. An ATS girl in the plotting room was sent down to the lower level. She said afterwards "I needed a map to get back up to our level."'

Ken Flint, Royal Signals, arrived in 1943.

We walked along rough-hewn greeny-grey passageways cut out of solid chalk. Occasionally the steady drip, drip of water not only permeated the ceilings but also our forage caps. The tunnels rambled gently downwards until we were at the top of a very steep flight of concrete steps, fortunately well lit and provided with a handrail of sorts. At the bottom was a maze of passages with fluorescent lights, festooned with pipes, cables and nozzles blowing out tangy salt air. It was in the small hours of one early morning in late 1943, while sitting with headphones on in front of the receiver concentrating on accurately recording the umpteenth of a never-ending stream of five-letter cipher 'groups', when the door was suddenly flung open dramatically and three or four face-blackened and tommy-gun-armed commandos

Behind the brick-built electric generator station at East Cliffe, Dover, lies the chalk spoil thrown out from the DUMPY underground HQ complex. Commandos climbed over the spoil to reach the unguarded entrance above when they infiltrated the DUMPY HQ in late 1943. *(Paul Wells)*

burst in. Their officer waved a pistol at us and ordered us to switch off and stop sending any more 'gen'. At that hour in the morning, with one's brain addled with radio atmospherics and interference, we did as we were told and sat back in our chairs obediently. We later learned they rampaged through the whole of the Combined HQ, but seemed unaware the Army cipher room was at the end of our radio bay. Had they known about it they could have boasted of its capture. Naturally there was never any mention of this mock attack, made by commandos who had climbed the cliff face and entered the tunnels by a back door. Rumour had it that the top brass had never considered the Germans would have gained entry by this difficult route.

The only casualty was a GPO technician working on wires in a small cubicle. A well-aimed thunder-flash exploded close to him with deafening results.

Engaging enemy shipping with artillery, but more especially the damage sustained by vessels and those recorded as sunk, was always a subject of much discussion in the castle canteens and billets. However, it was not until 20 January 1944 that the first sinking of any enemy ship was 'officially' notified for publication in the press. Churchill sent a message of congratulations addressed to the Commander, Coast Artillery, which read, 'Hearty congratulations on the good shooting of the Dover guns.' The vessel in question was the 7,000-ton *Munsterland*, and although the girls in the plotting room had been offered a prize of some sort for their efforts, they remained disappointed. When another large tanker was seen to disappear from the radar screens on 20 March 1944, the girls had a 'night out' on the town, although both Wanstone and South Foreland batteries wanted to claim the distinction of sinking it.

SEVEN

AN EERIE SILENCE

After the Second World War, just about everything moveable was cleared from casemate, ANNEXE and DUMPY. There was an eerie silence in the tunnels, broken only by the occasional exclamation of wonder, made by the odd visitor. The air within was still nasty but no longer blurred by the choking fumes which once hung like a toxic mist high up in the chalk ceilings during excavation. The fascination with Dover's tunnels is insatiable, perhaps centring on the gritty toil of the tunnellers or on the darkened abandoned vaults and chambers that were synonymous with the threat of war.

Winston Churchill as Lord Warden of the Cinque Ports inspects the troops at Dover Castle in 1946.

When the world stood poised on the edge of nuclear annihilation in the second half of the twentieth century, there were preparations for a Third World War. Subsequently, for fifty years the 'Cold War' became an undisputed fact that influenced the lives of everyone who lived through it, and which left its mark in so many different ways. Modern technology meant that some military hardware and, more especially, early-warning of a nuclear attack needed a sophisticated network of subterranean concrete bunkers out of sight of the enemy.

The mere thought of an unprovoked attack upon the United States, after the Pearl Harbor fiasco of 7 December 1941, became the embodiment of fear which would not go away. The result of this paranoia gave America the necessary impetus to develop scientific, military and industrial resources that were poised to defend its territory and its people. A highly sophisticated early-warning requirement had, over fifty years, spread like some cancerous growth around the world as well as the need to monitor every move the Soviets made.

In their underground command centres, men and women, protected and surrounded by the latest ferroconcrete, sought to observe the unstoppable nuclear missiles hell-bent on their destruction. Bunkers designed to protect a democratic government so that they could later re-emerge to rule the few survivors, were built at extreme costs and in secrecy.

Unwittingly, the Western World was drawn into this world of secrecy by the suggestion of 'mutual defence for the common good' syndrome. Inevitably the 'listening posts', fighter and

This recently installed GPO 1940s-style telephone switchboard tableau only requires the girls sitting at their units to confirm the authenticity.

bomber airfields, nuclear submarines and much more, were spread across the North Atlantic, Canada, Great Britain, France, Germany and Italy. In Great Britain there were, as a result of America's paranoia, dozens of subterranean bunkers built to protect key elements of the nation's military and administrative establishments. Dover's tunnels became one of them.

Deep underground these complex bunkers, large and small, built by an army of expert military and civilian tunnelling companies, have cost the taxpayer tens of millions of pounds, not only to build them but also to maintain them. Within these structures were the bunkers for regional governments, county councils, water board engineers, electricity engineers, telecommunications engineers and Royal Observer Corps volunteers. The whole gamut was thought to protect the British populace but, in reality, it was part of a more elaborate system that was to protect the United States.

Ever since 1936, the widespread development of radar, especially during the Second World War, inevitably led to the active and passive Air Defence of the Western Powers. The earliest equipment was only capable of detecting aircraft at medium altitude with the minimum degrees of accuracy, but was quite incapable of low-level accuracy. By 1941, however, a Ground Control Intercept (GCI) radar was developed under a completely new command structure and totally separate from the earlier functional command which, unfortunately, led to inter-command rivalry, and hindering the effective developments of the radar system until well into the 1960s.

The array of wireless aerials are seen here above Dover Castle in 1945.

Surprisingly, while the control and reporting systems had expanded during the Second World War, the financial and manpower demands were reduced to a minimum after the threat of German air attacks had receded. Even so, in the spring of 1944 there were 208 early-warning stations and thirty-three Ground Control Intercept stations, with twenty of the latter already reduced to care and maintenance. By 1945, a further eighteen on the east coast and all of the west coast had closed as well as most of the Chain Home Stations in the north-west.

Three years later, and with the inevitable tensions of the Cold War escalating, Great Britain was once again vulnerable to air attack. The operational radar systems still functioning were on the south and east coasts. Elsewhere most of the radar stations had been closed down and stripped of their equipment and were either under care and maintenance or had been abandoned.

In the immediate post-war period, the shape of British air defences was determined and would last at least another twenty years. The first report, made by the Chief of Staff, was issued as early as July 1945, under the title *Air Defence of Great Britain*. Another, published by Group Captain J. Cherry, later superseded this report, which drew attention to major weaknesses in the first report. Above all he suggested accomplishments for the future using new technology not yet developed. His report, however, made little impact on the Labour government of the day, for they had already imposed financial restraints upon any defence arrangements.

Following the Berlin Airlift of 1948, improvements of this country's air defence involved reopening some of the Second World War radar stations and even constructing new ones. It was primarily a quick solution to an otherwise thorny problem, providing an adequate radar system at a bearable cost within the two-year period.

The inadequacies of wartime equipment called for a more up-to-date system as a matter of extreme urgency, which brought about the 'Rotor Scheme' developed jointly by the Air Staff and the Ministry of Supply during the 1950s. Despite the urgency, the first Rotor was seen as a poor substitute until more powerful, high discrimination centimetric radar became available.

In view of the perceived seriousness of the international situation, Swingate's Chain Home site above Dover was overhauled and re-equipped under the largest defence capital expenditure ever undertaken in Britain. To maintain the necessary high level of air coverage from Portland Bill to Flamborough Head, twenty-eight Chain Home Extra Stations were restored. Fourteen new Chain Early-Warning (CEW) and Chain Home Extra Low (CHEL) stations, one of which was the St Margaret's station, were introduced.

Within the scope of the various reporting stations was the Anti-Aircraft Operations Room (AAOR), one of which was using the DUMPY tunnel system beneath Dover Castle. This unit was in immediate contact with the nearest Ground Control Intercept (GCI) at Sandwich which in turn was in contact with the Sector Operations Centre (SOC) at Kelvedon Hatch, Essex. Because the Rotor radar system relied on the old landline telephone system of reporting through many thousands of miles of telephone cable, deployment of GPO staff under the short-sighted government restrictions delayed the whole project. The visible evidence of a Rotor station being built was all-too-obvious to any casual observer, as huge depressions were necessary on open ground before any construction work was undertaken.

All sorts of delays were attendant on completion of these Rotor sites; cuts in capital expenditure meant a retardation of the rearmament programme and the metric equipment providing high air cover above 25,000ft was found, initially, to be susceptible to jamming.

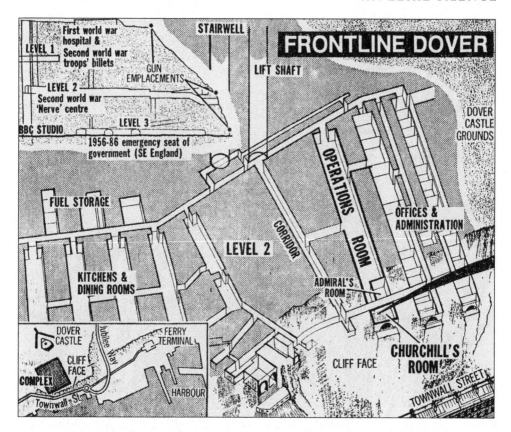

A plan of the complex beneath Dover Castle.

In the event, twelve American FPS-3 radar sets were purchased and, although Portland had been selected as the first to use them, the St Margaret's site was chosen for the prototype even before the groundwork had been completed. As a result the new equipment was temporarily housed in a wooden hut above surface and was actually operational on 16 March 1953. Before long, a new 10-centimetre long-range early-warning radar was developed which proved superior to the earlier equipment. Known as the 'Type 80 Mk1' it introduced an automatic plotting system but was not ready for installation until 1954.

Developments in radar and associated equipment became obsolete almost overnight. The Air Council approved the introduction of the Automatic Air Defence Information System (ADIS), Plan Position Indicators (PPIs) and the Kelvin Hughes Photographic Display Unit, which later was installed below the floor level in operations rooms. The installation date for the Type 80 Mk1 radar at St Margaret's was 8 September 1955, and it was soon realised that it was difficult to jam by conventional means existing at the time and, above all, it possessed a high resolution. Before long, however, rapid developments had moved electronics into the digital age, where

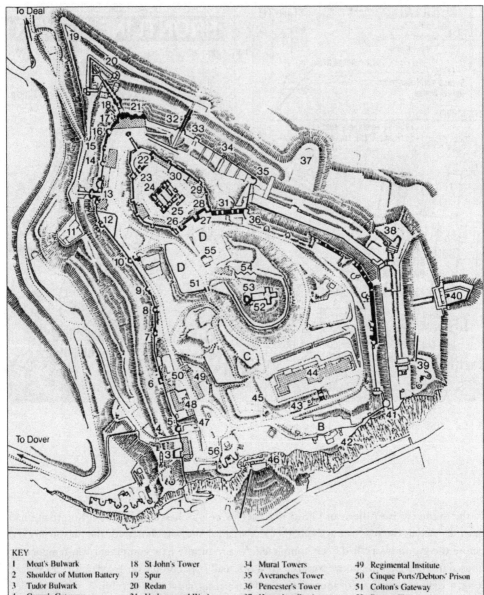

KEY

1	Moat's Bulwark	18	St John's Tower
2	Shoulder of Mutton Battery	19	Spur
3	Tudor Bulwark	20	Redan
4	Canon's Gateway	21	Underground Works
5	Rokesley's Tower	22	King's Gate Barbican
6	Fulbert of Dover's Tower	23	King's Gateway
7	Hurst's Tower	24	Keep
8	Say's Tower	25	Inner Bailey
9	Gatton's Tower	26	Palace Gateway
10	Peverell's Tower	27	Arthur's Gateway (site of)
11	Constable's Bastion	28	Keep Yard Barracks
12	Queen Mary's Tower	29	Arthur's Hall
13	Constable's Gateway/Tower	30	Keep Yard Barracks
14	Treasurer's Tower		(regimental museum)
15	Godsfoe's Tower	31	Bell Battery
16	Crevecoeur's Tower	32	Fitzwilliam Gateway
17	Norfolk Towers	33	Mural Towers

34	Mural Towers	49	Regimental Institute
35	Averanches Tower	50	Cinque Ports'/Debtors' Prison
36	Pencester's Tower	51	Colton's Gateway
37	Horseshoe Bastion	52	Roman Pharos
38	Hudson's Bastion		(lighthouse)
39	East Demi-Bastion	53	St Mary-en-Castro
40	East Arrow Bastion		Church
41	(site of) Radar	54	Four-gun Battery
42	Port War Signal Station/	55	Well
	Admiralty Lookout	56	Shot Yard Battery
43	Stairs to Cliff Casemates	A	Guilford Battery (site of)
44	Officers' Mess	B	Cliff Block Hospital (site of)
45	Long Gun Magazine	C	Saluting Battery (site of)
46	Cliff Casemate Barracks		and Beacon
47	Powder Magazine	D	Palace Green Barracks
48	Royal Garrison		& Married Quarters (site of)
	Artillery Barracks	E	Well Tower (site of)

the transfer of information, and perhaps more significantly, the invention of the Carcinotron Valve, was to effectively negate any advantage the Rotor radar system had.

Technology ousted the Rotor system, so nuclear physics and the ever-changing international situation ensured its demise. Radar protection had been assured under the Rotor radar, giving solid air cover both over land and sea, especially at low-level and medium altitudes. However, when the USA detonated the first thermonuclear weapon ('H' bomb) in October 1952, this weapon of unimaginable horror inevitably hastened the demise of Anti-Aircraft Command, whose very existence had been sitting on a knife-edge since it was realised that anti-aircraft guns of any calibre would never bring down or get anywhere near high-flying subsonic and supersonic aircraft.

The existence of the 'H' bomb had changed the whole concept of war, so much so that the changed circumstances meant that the existing Rotor defence system was unable to fulfil its role and became obsolete at a stroke. These rapid changes had occurred before the whole system had been finally completed and handed over to Fighter Command.

The St Margaret's Rotor (CEW) station, near Dover, was finally decommissioned in 1960. Site maintenance continued, however, until 1982, at about which time the surface buildings were demolished and the underground bunker sealed from prying eyes.

The Anti-Aircraft Operations Room (AAOR) beneath Dover Castle in DUMPY, although built to a standard design, did not need a massive rebuild, only the blast-proof steel doors required at the entrances and exits, with steel plates protecting the grilles over the ventilation shafts which served the main operations rooms and offices. Inside were the usual two-storey operations room, which was overlooked by a balcony on three sides, fitted with curved perplex glazing that gave an unobstructed view of the plotting table below. Corridors around the outside of the operations room gave access to the offices and cubicles, below was housed the generator unit providing emergency electrical power and next to it was the forced-air ventilation room. On the lower floor level and to the rear of the operations room was housed the radio room and GPO telecommunications equipment. After the demise of the Anti-Aircraft Command in 1955, the DUMPY AAOR was abandoned.

Before the subsequent change of name for the Civil Defence in 1968, plans were already in place to form a Control Government War Headquarters at Corsham, Wiltshire, and a chain of Regional Seats of Government bunkers in the remaining counties. The ethics of providing heavily protected bunkers for an elite minority while the rest of the population was consigned to nuclear annihilation, allowed the Civil Defence commitment to diminish beyond recovery. In 1957 a Defence White Paper suggested that in the nuclear age the Civil Defence could have no realistic rescue and recovery role as it had possessed in the Second World War. The true purpose of the Civil Defence was not to ensure the survival of as large a proportion of the population as possible, but to ensure the survival of government whatever may befall the country.

Up until the 1970s and beyond, most of the infrastructure changes regarding the early-warning and monitoring systems reflected the government's need for financial restraint, to dispense with the obsolete and render more efficient whatever remained.

It was only during the Cold War period that the DUMPY complex was reinstated to form a Regional Seat of Government in the likely event of nuclear war. The whole DUMPY complex, as an operations centre, was reintroduced but on a much larger scale and with more modern equipment. Included was a complete BBC studio whose signals would use the underground cable systems still connected to the two original transmitters outside the castle.

Hidden behind a veil of anonymity, the Regional Seat of Government at Dover Castle was no more secret to the local populace than was their involvement with the Civil Defence Corps. Men and women, family and friends, not only knew of its existence but allowed the fact of their involvement to permeate conversation likely to induce a certain awe and wonderment. The only secret lay in the latest technology hidden inside the tunnels where the steel and concrete structure below ground was simply to protect it against blast and radiation. The new centre with its many planning rooms remained in use until the early 1980s when, just before new work was about to start, it was decided to move the Regional Seat to Crowborough.

A cynical view perhaps, but there is always political value in the art of secrecy more especially if you confound your enemies into believing you have weapons of unimaginable power and, at the same time, keeping the domestic front in ignorance. It is common knowledge that governments often find it advantageous to uphold the aura of secrecy surrounding a particular site long after its original purpose has faded from memory. After all, it distracts attention from the real issue of secrecy surrounding its successor.

When the Cold War ended with the collapse of the Soviet Union, the majority of the local government bunkers in existence were abandoned. By the end of the decade all regional government headquarters were gone, sold off or left to decay. Those few which still remain today are one or two Command, Control and Communication bunkers and the still-secret Emergency Government War Headquarters at Spring Quarry, near Corsham, Wiltshire.

Removed from the secret list, DUMPY, as well as the rest of the castle, is now run by English Heritage as a tourist attraction. Interestingly, the Ministry of Defence papers, and others relating to these underground bunkers, most of which have been either sold to private companies or abandoned, almost without exception, are closed for at least one hundred years.

APPENDIX I

Statutes of Dover Castle

The life of the castle garrison can be gleaned from these excerpts from an ancient surviving document written in Norman French. This is but a fragment but will throw some light upon the scene. It was promulgated in the reign of King Henry III and later was declared by Sir Stephen de Pencestre who had been appointed Constable of Dover Castle in 1267.

At sunset the bridge shall be drawn, and the gates shut; afterwards the guard shall be mounted by twenty warders on the castle wall.

Any warder found outside the walls or otherwise off his guard shall be put in the Donjon prison and punished besides in body and goods at the constable's discretion since for that watch the castle was trusted to him, not to be surprised through his fault.
After the last mount, two sergeants shall turn out of their houses to serve as chief guards. They shall make continual rounds within the castle to visit the warders on the walls and see that they right loyally keep watch without going to sleep, by reason that they have the constable's leave to sleep as much as they like in the daytime.

It is established by ancient rule that if a chief guard discover a warder asleep, he shall take something from him as he lies, or carry away his staff, or cut a piece out of part of his clothes to witness against him in case the warder should deny having been asleep and shall lose his day's wage.

And if it happen that the sergeant will not make such arrest, for pity's sake, or even for life's sake, then he shall be brought before the constable and be sentenced to prison 'dur en fort'; after that he shall be led to the great gate in presence of the garrison, and there expelled the castle; besides he shall lose his wage and forfeit all his chattels found within the castle walls.

Either sergeant or warder using vile language shall be brought before the constable who shall have the matter considered, and the offence fairly enquired into. He who was in the wrong shall lose his day's pay, if the constable so wills.

If the sergeant or warder strike another with the flat hand, he shall be liable to a fine as high as five shillings, and shall for the rest be held at the mercy of the court. If he strikes with his fist he shall be liable to a fine as high as ten shillings, and be at the mercy of the court. If a sergeant or warder wound another the fine shall be as high as fifteen shillings and the offender shall forfeit his station in the castle, if the constable so adjudge.

Because the castle is out of common jurisdiction, it is ordained that at every quarter of the year shall the whole garrison be mustered in the presence of the constable, and any shall then before him be addressed and reprehended who may be accused of any notable crime, which is out of right by Holy Church be dealt with. And if the constable find himself in a perplexity thereupon, he may take council of some parson of Holy Church who shall advise what to do in such case.

There shall be one sergeant and one guard elected in full garrison assembled who shall be sworn to 'leal' keeping of the light in Holy Church which is not burning inside the chancel (i.e., at the Soldiers Altar).

And because the priests are sworn on their consciences to keep 'leal' watch over the chancel lights, if any one of them knows of the others doing other than they ought, he shall report them and accuse them before the constable, unless indeed they be willing to inflict penance on themselves, and then he may excuse them.

Reliques [sic] are appointed to be shown and especially such as are of the true cross shall be brought out every Friday and placed on the high altar for the ringing of prime the end of high mass.

They shall be open to all who wish to visit them for the honour of God, and the benefit of the chapel. One of the chaplains or clerk, vested in surplice, shall remain by the Reliques and may shew [sic] and explain them and pronounce absolution to those who desire it.

At all great feasts of the year, that is at the feasts of Our Lord and of Our Lady, St John, of St Peter and Paul, and of all saints, and such as are double and solemn shall afterwards mass be sung. And on the vigils shall be grand singing and afterwards at the procession and sequence at matins and vespers shall be Te Deum, Laus Deo and Gloria in Excelsis.

Every Sunday after mass, holy bread shall be given in the chancel to all who have attended the festivals, marriages or sermons in the preceding week.

The priests are to pray for the recovery of the Holy Land, the success of Christianity, the king and royal family, the barons of the realm, the constable and garrison.

The rector, or one of the chaplains at his request, after the gospel for their day is to deliver a discourse to the entire garrison, or to as many who attended high mass.

[Another statute of the same period says] If the king arrives unexpectedly in the night, the gates shall not be opened to him, but he shall go to the postern called King's Gate, towards the north and there the constable and those who accompany him, may admit the king and a certain number of his suite. When the king is admitted he has the command, and in the morning, when it is full day, he may admit the remainder of his company.

APPENDIX II

Sir Edward Guleford was ordered to supply sustenance for Henry VIII for one month. The details are recorded below.

700 quarters of wine
10 tuns of French and Gaston wine
6 butts of sweet wine
560 tuns of ale
340 beeves at forty shillings
4200 mutton at five shillings
800 veals at five shillings
80 hogheads of grease
Salt and fresh fish at £300
Spices at £400
Diapers at £300
4,000 pounds of wax white lights at £26 13s 4d
Poultry at £1,300
Pewter vessels at £300
Pans and spits at £200
5,600 quarters of coal
Tallwood and billets at £200
Sables at £200

APPENDIX III

Constables of Dover Castle

Since 1227 the appointment of Lord Warden of the Cinque Ports has carried with it, either in law or by force of arms, the constableship of Dover Castle.

1067 Odo, Bishop of Bayeux	1660 Prince James, Duke of York
1084 John de Fiennes	1702 George, Prince of Denmark
1150 Prince Eustace	1778 Earl of Guilford
1202 Hubert de Burgh/ Stephen Langdon	1792 William Pitt
1223 William d'Avranches	1829 Duke of Wellington
1258 Richard de Grey	1860 Viscount Palmerston
1263 Prince Edmund	1866 Earl of Granville
1265 Prince Edward	1891 Marquis of Dufferin and Ava
1267 William Clynton	1895 Marquis of Salisbury
1359 Baron Beauchamp	1904 Lord Curzon of Keddleston
1409 Henry, Prince of Wales	1905 George, Prince of Wales
1493 Henry, Duke of York	(King George V)
1558 William Brook	1908 Earl of Brassey
1625 Duke of Buckingham	1913 Earl of Beauchamp

BIBLIOGRAPHY

History of Dover Castle Rev: plans and etchings, William Drell, 1760

History of Dover Castle (Roman, Saxon, Norman), 1787

Dover: England's gate, etchings of town and castle, 1880

The Church and Fortress of Dover Castle. Rev, John Puckle, MA, 1864

History of Dover's Castle town and port of Dover Rev, S.P.H. Statham, 1899

Dover Castle, V.A. Hundlery, 1925

The Saxon Shore and Fortress, E.G.J. Amos & R.E.M. Wheeler, 1930

The Organisation of War under Edward III 1338–62, H.J. Hewitt, Manchester University Press, 1966

Dover Castle, Jonathan Coad, English Heritage, 1995

Hellfire Corner, Jonathan Coad, English Heritage, 1993

Histoire des Ducs de Normandie et des Rois d'Angleterre, Michel, F. (ed.), Paris, 1840

ACKNOWLEDGEMENTS

I am indebted to the following for all their help.

English Heritage
Maggie Smith
John Iverson
Bob Hollingsbee
John Guy
Robin Brooks

Other titles published by The History Press

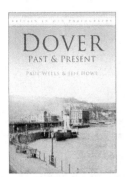

Dover Past & Present
PAUL WELLS & JEFF HOWE

ISBN 978-0-7524-5192-3

This fascinating book is a guide to Dover's history, using over 150 images to illustrate how the town has developed into its present form. Recalling a bygone era, this volume explores Dover's most important features and attractions, and shows how they have evolved through several generations. Comparing modern photographs with rare images from the past, this collection documents the many changes that have taken place, but also includes the familiar sights that remain unspoilt by modern progress.

Haunted Dover
LORRAINE SENCICLE

ISBN 978-0-7524-4859-6

The historic port of Dover has had its fair share of waifs and strays travelling through it over the course of many years. The castle, pubs, and the labyrinth of subterranean chambers beneath the white cliffs host a variety of ghouls and spectres, and this spine-tingling book will fascinate anyone who dares to read it.

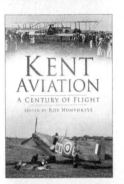

Kent Aviation
A CENTURY OF FLIGHT

ROY HUMPHREYS

ISBN 978-0-7524-5121-3

Using over 350 photographs, Roy Humphreys tells the story of civil and military aviation in Kent. From the excitement and glamour of early pioneers to the RFC and RNAS in the First World War; from the 'golden age' of flying in the 1920s and '30s to the airfields of the Second World War and the present day – all facets of aviation history are covered.

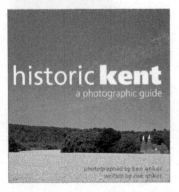

Historic Kent
A PHOTOGRAPHIC GUIDE

BEN & ZOE ANKER

ISBN 978-0-7509-4320-8

Although there have been many books about Kent, none has been as uniquely designed or as purposefully photographed as this. *Historic Kent* is a contemporary introduction to much of what the county has to offer – from cathedrals and castles to coastlines and country gardens. It is a journey around the county which is sure to appeal to residents who know and love the 'Garden of England' and to tourists discovering it for the first time.

Visit our website and discover thousands of other History Press books.

www.thehistorypress.co.uk

Made in the USA
Columbia, SC
18 January 2020